Personalisation in Social Work

Second edition

ALI GARDNER

Series Editors: Jonathan Parker and Greta Bradley

 SAGE | LearningMatters

Los Angeles | London | New Delhi
Singapore | Washington DC

Learning Matters
An imprint of SAGE Publications Ltd
1 Oliver's Yard
55 City Road
London EC1Y 1SP

SAGE Publications Inc.
2455 Teller Road
Thousand Oaks, California 91320

SAGE Publications India Pvt Ltd
B 1/I 1 Mohan Cooperative Industrial Area
Mathura Road
New Delhi 110 044

SAGE Publications Asia-Pacific Pte Ltd
3 Church Street
#10–04 Samsung Hub
Singapore 049483

Editor: Luke Block
Production controller: Chris Marke
Project management: Deer Park Productions,
Tavistock, Devon
Marketing manager: Tamara Navaratnam
Cover design: Wendy Scott
Typeset by: C&M Digitals (P) Ltd, Chennai, India
Printed by: Henry Ling Limited at The Dorset Press,
Dorchester, DT1 1HD

Library of Congress Control Number: 2013954556

British Library Cataloguing in Publication Data

A catalogue record for this book is available from
the British Library

ISBN 978-1-4462-6879-7 (pbk)
ISBN 978-1-4462-6878-0

Contents

Acknowledgements

I would like to thank three people who shared their time, stories and kindness to make this book possible. These three people demonstrate the possibilities of personalisation and their determination is something to be admired. I would like to thank the two other contributors to this edition, David Gaylard, for his willingness to share and discuss the contents of this book at length, and Natalie Robinson, for being the kind of student that makes teaching so easy by nodding so enthusiastically from the back of a classroom and for her honest engagement in this process. I would also like to thank all my colleagues in the social work department at Manchester Metropolitan University for their support and encouragement.

Thank you to Ken Stapleton, Karen Saville and Gavin Croft for sharing their abundance of knowledge and infectious enthusiasm and positivity towards personalisation even at times when the cards are stacked against them.

Finally I would like to thank my family, Des, Dad and Sue, for their patience and proofreading, and last, but not least, my two special stars Grace and Hope for allowing me to use the computer from time to time, making me cups of tea and keeping me topped up with cuddles.

David Gaylard would like to thank Paul Tavender, senior social work practitioner, Hampshire County Council, and Viv Killner, senior social work practitioner, West Sussex County Council.

About the author and contributors

Ali Gardner is a Senior Lecturer in Social Work at Manchester Metropolitan University where she teaches on a number of modules including law and social work, working with disabled people and personalisation. Ali has worked as a social worker and policy officer in the field of adult social care. She has been involved in the national development of policy and practice relating to personalisation, working alongside Social Care Institute of Excellence (SCIE), Think Local Act Personal (TLAP) and Skills for Care (SfC) and has written the personalisation curriculum guide for the College of Social Work.

David Gaylard has been Senior Lecturer in Social Work at the University of Chichester since 2006. Prior to his current post he was a team manager in one of the personalisation pilot sites and has worked in a range of statutory adult social work departments in Hertfordshire, the London boroughs of Wandsworth and Kensington and Chelsea, in West Sussex and in Portsmouth. During this period he also qualified as an Approved Social Worker and Practice Teacher. David has trained and worked in the NHS as a registered general nurse at St George's Hospital, London. His research interests include mental ill health, adult safeguarding and diversity in practice. David is currently undertaking a doctorate in social work at the University of Sussex, examining personalisation under austerity.

Natalie Robinson is a newly qualified social worker who studied her undergraduate degree at Manchester Metropolitan University. Natalie's interest in personalisation came from years of working in various different support worker roles supporting children, young people and adults with learning disabilities. Natalie's passion for personalisation was ignited when she undertook the elective in her final year of study. It also came from her keen interest of the historical context of how people with disabilities have been treated by society over the decades. Since qualifying Natalie has kept herself updated with the personalisation agenda. Natalie has worked as an onsite supervisor mentoring new social work students and in the future she hopes to undertake the practice educator training. Natalie's dream is to one day set up her own social enterprise that is purely based upon personalisation principles.

Introduction

This book is written primarily for social work students to improve their understanding of the personalisation agenda. It will support students in developing their practice in a way that embeds the ideologies, values, principles, theories, policies and processes informing this agenda. A central focus to this book is a belief that personalisation is about thinking and doing. The reader will be continually encouraged to consider their own underlying assumptions and values in relation to notions of social care and welfare. In addition to highlighting several success stories through service user narrative, the book will explore some of the challenges and dilemmas social workers are likely to encounter in supporting service users to direct their own support. This fundamental understanding and critical reflection will enable the reader to develop congruence between values and social work practice at all times.

It is fundamentally important that practitioners understand why and how this working context has emerged. The book provides a brief historical sweep of welfare in Britain leading up to the government's commitment to this agenda in the form of the *Putting people first* concordat (HM Government, 2007). The reader will be encouraged to critically analyse and evaluate how changing policies and practices are likely to impact on their own role as practitioners as the personalisation agenda unfolds.

The book will support qualifying students to make the transition from theory to practice. A new chapter (7), specifically focuses on the new Professional Capabilities Framework (PCF), supporting students in their transition from academia to practice within a personalisation context. The chapter examines the shift away from the social work role being described as one of 'manager' to that of an 'enabler' within the self-directed support model. The book, however, will support the reader to see that values, theories and methods underpinning the personalisation agenda are very familiar to social work. Good practice has always involved putting the individual first, and values such as respect and self-determination have also been adopted as key philosophies for social workers (BASW, 2002). Building on this assumption, the text will support students in considering how to demonstrate their professional capability while on placement by mapping it to the PCF. In this way the book will also be useful to practice educators supporting students working in environments where personalisation and self-directed support are central to their work.

The book may also support qualified practitioners and those engaging in Continued Professional Development (CPD) activities, working in new personalised environments, to reflect critically on their own practice. Several of the activities provided encourage the reader to return to the fundamental values of social work. In this sense the book provides opportunities for qualified social workers to consider the extent to which their own practice and values have been shaped by traditional models of social care and welfare. Chapters 2 and 3 offer an opportunity to reflect on the transition from care management to self-directed support and explore the subtle, yet significant, ideological differences in these two approaches.

The book can be used at many different levels. First, it can be used to simply understand how and why the personalisation agenda emerged. It can also be used to learn or familiarise oneself with new ways of working by reflecting on examples of existing practice and developments. Finally, the book can also be used to encourage students and practitioners to engage with more radical forms of learning by challenging practice at a more fundamental level and addressing issues within an anti-discriminatory and anti-oppressive framework of practice.

Book structure

Chapter 1: Personalisation – Where did it come from?

The first chapter traces the influences leading to the emergence of the current agenda. This includes an analytical examination of the history of social welfare. The chapter reflects on the impact of the user-led movements and its influence in relation to emerging legislation and policy relating to self-directed support. By the end of this chapter you will have a clearer understanding of the policy and service delivery context within which personalisation now exists.

Chapter 2: Personalisation – A value base for practice

The focus of this chapter is to develop congruence between social work values and social work practice. The chapter considers concepts of paternalism versus citizenship and the deserving versus the undeserving in relation to models of social welfare, and how anti-discriminatory and anti-oppressive models of practice can be developed within a personalisation context. Finally, the chapter poses the question: is personalisation a new paradigm or simply a repackaged model of social welfare?

Chapter 3: Personalisation in practice

This chapter critically examines the current context of personalisation in practice. It focuses on changing ideology and models of support from the traditional care management model to the self-directed model of support. Focusing on the role and challenges faced by social workers practising in the current climate of shrinking resources, the chapter explores the key stages of self-assessment, supporting planning and review.

Chapter 4: Service user groups and personalisation

In this chapter we consider current practice and developments within different service user groups. This will focus on the 2013 Personal Budgets Outcomes and Evaluation

Tool (POET) survey. In addition the chapter explores some of the opportunities and challenges presented within the emerging areas of development in relation to the personalisation agenda. These include:

- health
- housing and homelessness
- the criminal justice system
- disabled children.

Chapter 5: Service user narrative

This chapter provides an opportunity to learn from three individuals who have used personal and individual budgets. The aim of the chapter is to reflect on their individual and collective experiences. The purpose of using the three individual accounts is to provide some insight into the diverse ways individuals have designed and managed their support. Activities are used to support students to reflect on both the diverse and common experiences of individuals. The chapter encourages the reader to think about the social work role in supporting people to use their own expertise to control and direct their support.

Chapter 6: Safeguarding and personalisation

The chapter addresses some of the key tensions that exist for service users, practitioners, managers and the government in promoting choice and control while reducing risk and harm. The chapter explores both the ideological and the practical debates surrounding the safeguarding agenda. Case examples and activities are used to aid debate, learning and challenge in relation to this discourse. The chapter reflects on emerging research in relation to safeguarding and personalisation and encourage the reader to evaluate findings critically.

Chapter 7: Preparing for practice and the Professional Capabilities Framework (PCF)

This chapter focuses on supporting students, academics and practice educators to understand personalisation within the context of the recently developed Professional Capabilities Framework (PCF). The introduction of a mapping tool will enable students to identify and demonstrate evidence that will contribute towards their progression from the level of entry through to the qualification and beyond.

Chapter 8: Personalisation – A newly qualified perspective

This chapter is from the perspective of a newly qualified practitioner who provides a narrative account of her journey from student to practitioner. Reflecting on the personal and professional challenges she has encountered, she aims to provide an understanding of what social work means to her within the context of personalisation.

Learning features

As with other books in this series, case examples, activities, reflection points, research summaries and signposting to additional reading will be used to aid the learning process. The book is intended to be interactive. An understanding of personalisation requires a commitment to engaging with the values, theories, ideologies and histories that have influenced its development. As a student and a practitioner it is important that you are able and willing to reflect on your own thoughts, experiences and practices in a critical way (Jones, 2009; Quinney, 2006), but, more importantly, that you are willing to change fundamental assumptions, perceptions or beliefs and ultimately practice, as a result of that reflection.

Chapter 1

Personalisation – Where did it come from?

Ali Gardner

ACHIEVING A SOCIAL WORK DEGREE

This chapter will help you to develop the following capabilities from the Professional Capabilities Framework:

- **Knowledge**
  Apply knowledge of social sciences, law and social work practice theory.

- **Critical reflection and analysis**
  Apply critical reflection and analysis to inform and provide a rationale for professional decision-making.

- **Contexts and organisations**
  Engage with, inform, and adapt to changing contexts that shape practice. Operate effectively within your own organisational frameworks and contribute to the development of services and organisations. Operate effectively within multi-agency and inter-professional settings.

It will also introduce you to the following standards as set out in the 2008 social work subject benchmark statement.

5.1.2   **The service delivery context.**

Introduction

Personalisation was officially introduced in government policy in December 2007 with the publication of the *Putting people first* concordat (HM Government, 2007). It set out the shared aims and values required to guide the transformation of adult social care in order to transform people's experience of local support and services. Personalisation, however, is not specific to social care and started as a cross-government agenda in 2003. The emerging ideas were articulated in the 2004 Demos report, *Personalisation through participation: A new script for public services* (Leadbeater, 2004). In this report, author Charles Leadbeater described a society where service users would be placed at the heart of services, enabling them to become *participants in the design and delivery of services* (p. 19). He argued that by mobilising millions of people as co-producers of the public good they value, services will be more effective. He went on to identify five different meanings of personalisation.

- Providing people with customer-friendly versions of existing services.
- Giving people who use services more say in how these services are run, once they have access to them.
- Giving people who use services a more direct say in how money is spent on services.
- Enabling people who use services to become co-designers and co-producers of services.
- Enabling self-organisation by society.

Leadbeater (2004) describes the last two meanings as *deeper personalisation* in that it is not simply a matter of modifying services but challenging the ideology of the relationship between the state and the service users and changing whole systems of the way people work together. In his powerful concluding comments, these senti-ments are very clear: *In an open, self-organising society, government has to become molecular; it has to get into the bloodstream of society, not impose change or deliver solutions from outside* (Leadbeater, 2004, p. 89). While the Demos report was tar-geted at all areas of public policy, the opportunity and connections for social care to build on this platform of thinking were clear and went on to shape the policy and practice of social care from this point onwards.

Personalisation through participation embodied the sentiments of several different strands of ideology, theory, policy and practice throughout the history of social care. In order to understand this journey, a brief overview of the history is necessary to appreciate the following changes in social care.

- The relationship between service user and the state.
- The role of the state.
- The move from institutional to independent living.
- The voices of those using services.
- Policy, legislation and government thinking.

Perhaps the most comprehensive way to do this is for you to embark on a virtual jour-ney and follow the timeline of social care thinking, policy and practice.

Nineteenth century

Social work first emerged as an activity around 1869 with the development of the Charity Organisation Society (COS) (Lewis, 1995; Glasby and Littlechild, 2009) with a belief that individual casework would be able to clearly assess whether a person was worthy or unworthy of assistance. The premise of its role lay in the fundamental belief that poverty was largely caused by individual and moral failings – by *feck-lessness and thriftlessness*. COS officers would determine whether an individual was deserving or undeserving. Those deemed deserving would be eligible for charitable resources while those deemed undeserving would be sent to the workhouse. This professional role was made possible by the introduction of the Poor Law Amendment Act in 1834 which was driven by the government's determination to underpin the operation of its provisions with a clear ideological statement of the distinction between the deserving and undeserving (Englander, 1998).

Prior to the Amendment Act in 1834, local parishes had been the focus of the relief for the poor. In 1601 the Act of Elizabeth laid down that each parish was to be responsible for the maintenance of its own poor. The parish administered support to the poor which was funded by a compulsory poor rate levied at those living in the community (Marshall, 1985). In this sense the local parish was seen as a unit of government, and relief of the poor was not seen as an issue that central government should intervene in.

Around the early 1800s the cost of relief had been rising for between 30 and 40 years, yet the results were not improving. Disgruntled with the constant burden, in the early 1830s local taxpayers made their complaints known and outbreaks of rural violence made it clear that urgent reform was essential (Edsall, 1971). Opinion in Parliament, however, was divided as to how the Poor Law system could be improved. The main question preoccupying many members of Parliament was whether it was right for the state to take some responsibility in such matters.

The Poor Law Amendment Act of 1834 was introduced, taking the power out of the hands of the parishes and placing it into the hands of central authority. *It brought in professionalism in administration where there had been amateurism and it represented an uncompromising attitude to poverty* (Marshall, 1985, p. 23).

A key characteristic of the Poor Law Amendment Act 1934 was to make dependence on relief as unattractive as possible and it was hoped that the ultimate threat of incarceration in the oppressive Victorian workhouses would achieve this (Buck and Smith, 2003).

The realities of the workhouse were well documented to the community to ensure people did not become idle. Guardians of the workhouses were advised by the central authority to create settings that were *positively repellent* (Englander, 1998, p. 32). Rising at 5 a.m. followed by prayer, little food and hard labour then to bed at 8 p.m. meant conditions were tough and relentless. Mindful that some taxpayers might worry that building and running the workhouse would impose an expense on them, a self-financing 'pauper management plan' saw that all residents of the workhouse would have to work to pay off the cost of their maintenance. Local residents were also empowered to apprehend anybody found begging and to bring them to the workhouse. For their trouble, they would be paid 20 shillings, which would be added onto the account of the 'beggars tab' (Sandel, 2010, p. 36).

Resistance to the Poor Law and the regime of the workhouse started to emerge around the mid-1930s. At first in the north of England and largely on the back of the factory reform campaign, popular leaders adopted the resistance to the Poor Law as, essentially, one more aspect of a wider struggle (Edsall, 1971). Riots were commonplace as the working class showed their dissatisfaction and bitter resentment of the workhouse regime (Chinn, 1995).

ACTIVITY **1.1**

The terms 'deserving' and 'undeserving' were widely used in the nineteenth century to determine who should receive resources or services.

- *Do you think these terms are still part of current social work practice?*
- *Can you think of examples where people are still classified in this way either by the state or society?*

COMMENT

It could be argued that there are still many examples where explicit or implicit discretion is used to decide whether a service should be provided. For example, an individual using drugs or alcohol presenting him/herself at Casualty on a busy Friday night may be treated with less compassion than a disabled person who has experienced a severe seizure, yet both could be presenting similar symptoms. In social work we like to think of ourselves as working in a non-judgemental way but it is likely that aspects of our work will be influenced by slotting people into categories of deserving and undeserving.

1940s – The post-war years

The Poor Law was finally abolished in 1948 with the introduction of the welfare state along with the National Assistance Act 1948, establishing a national scheme of social security benefits and legislation to provide welfare services for older and disabled people. A key characteristic of this legislation was the distinction between financial support and welfare services. The National Assistance Act 1948 established a National Assistance Board to deal with the financial welfare governed by national rules while the responsibility of welfare services was delegated to local authorities. This separation was welcomed as it helped to remove the stigma of the old Poor Law and social workers could work with individuals without having to first determine whether they were deserving of that support (Jordan, 1974, in Glasby and Littlechild, 2009).

Reflecting on this point, Glasby and Littlechild (2009) suggest that this attempt to distance social work from cash payments to those in need may be partly responsible for practitioners' subsequent failure to address poverty issues. This is potentially important in relation to the later development of direct payments and personal budgets which would call for social workers to re-engage with linking financial and welfare resources in supporting service users. Glasby and Littlechild suggest the involvement of social workers in making payments to service users is a fundamental shift in the nature of their profession and may go some way to explaining why some social services departments have been slow to take up direct payments.

Defining welfare

While it is difficult to define a welfare state precisely, the definition provided by Lowe (1999, in Powell and Hewitt, 2002) describes a welfare state as one which provides a minimum income to individuals and families, provides security to those falling into crisis and provides all citizens without distinction of status or class the best services available in relation to an agreed range of services. It was the universality of provision that made the welfare state something new and different. Prior to this, local welfare systems had varied from place to place. One of the key characteristics of the welfare state is the relationship it created between the state and the individual. The Beveridge report in 1942 firmly located the role of the state in administering and organising support and resources to individuals. At the same time welfare subjects were seen as citizens rather than paupers or non-citizens associated with the Poor Law (Marshall, 1963). It is interesting to note that this notion of citizenship was part of Beveridge's vision, as the Disabled People's Movement later criticised the government for creating a welfare system which denied their civil rights and failed to treat them as citizens. Further criticism, although from a different perspective, later came from right-wing critics who felt that the state should be 'rolled back' in favour of an 'opportunity state' whereby individuals would take more responsibility to create better conditions for themselves (Powell and Hewitt, 2002, p. 39). The question of how far a government should involve itself with such matters continues to divide government thinking.

ACTIVITY **1.2**

- *Think about any aspect of the welfare state. You might choose health, social care, housing or education, for example.*
- *Try to identify both the advantages and disadvantages of the state being involved in your chosen example.*
- *You don't have to agree with all the reasons but it will help you develop an awareness of the economic, social and political perspectives that impact on social policy. For example, you might choose free school meals.*

Advantages

- *Good healthy meals provided for the child.*
- *Helps the child concentrate and achieve more out of education.*
- *Doesn't take money out of a tight family budget.*
- *Child will be more able to participate in sporting activities which will improve health and well-being.*

Disadvantages

- *The child feels stigmatised and is teased because of his/her social status.*
- *Disincentive for parents to provide healthy balanced diet.*

(Continued)

(Continued)

- *Child may be limited by choice – school meals cannot be tailored to his/her exact preference.*
- *Child grows up with the belief that the state will always provide – may limit aspirations.*
- *Costly exercise to administer for the government, local authority and school.*

COMMENT

The example you used probably demonstrated the complexities involved in deciding how far the state should intervene. You may have identified some clear benefits of state involvement but you may also have noted some negative consequences. In making decisions about the level of intervention, the government must balance several factors including financial impact and benefit, predicted outcome and not forgetting public perception in order to remain popular with the electorate.

The 1960s and 1970s

Out of the civil rights movement of the 1960s and 1970s, which questioned the way power was used and distributed in society, disabled people started to express their demand for social change by setting up organisations run by disabled people. Unconvinced that the state had shaken off the legacy of the old Poor Law and concerned that the state controlled and dictated how welfare resources were distributed, they sought to change medical-model-based thinking of disability (Swain et al., 1993). Disabled people characterised the old Poor Law as being an administrative model in their dealings with people with physical and other impairments, viewing them as a problem which required paid officials to assess, define, classify, register, administer and control. This is an important discussion, as the administrative model set the direction and tone for future disability policy and can still be viewed in current practice and policy (Davies, 1998).

In the early 1970s the Union of the Physically Impaired against Segregation (UPIAS) paved the way for a civil rights struggle when it redefined disability as a socially constructed phenomenon:

> *The disadvantage or restriction of ability caused by a contemporary social organisation which takes little or no account of people who have physical impairments and thus excludes them from participation in the mainstream of social activities.*

> (UPIAS, 1976, p. 14)

Around the same time the anti-psychiatry/mental health survivor movement was beginning to mobilise itself. Again critical of the medical model in mental health, service users campaigned in particular for the closure of long-stay psychiatric hospitals, another legacy of the old workhouse. This began to challenge existing perceptions of the institution as an appropriate model of care. A new piece of legislation, the Chronically Sick and Disabled Persons Act 1970, was introduced, placing a duty on local authorities to provide care and support services to disabled people to enable them to continue living in the community.

The 1980s

During the 1980s the Conservative government introduced a number of measures to tighten up the criteria for benefits in an attempt to eliminate the perceived 'dependency culture' and move to an individualistic, consumer-based approach to social care (McDonald, 2006). In 1981 the British Council of Disabled People (BCODP) was formed. Central to its strategy was the drive to increase the number of organisations controlled by disabled people. Viewing disability as a consequence of society's unwillingness to remove social barriers so disabled people could be equal citizens in mainstream social life, they set out to challenge the oppressive structures which stood in the way of their liberation.

The Social Security Act 1986 replaced Supplementary Benefit with Income Support, which had stricter eligibility criteria. In effect this piece of legislation financially disadvantaged many disabled people (Hudson, 1988). In response, the Disabled People's Movement successfully lobbied the government to introduce a new Independent Living Fund (ILF) in 1988 for people on low incomes who had to pay for personal care. The fund was only ever intended as a five-year transitional payment for those directly affected by the changes in the benefit rules. Disabled people, however, reported greater autonomy and clearly favoured and publicised the positive effects of the ILF (Kestenbaum, 1993). Threatened by the rising cost of the ILF, the government introduced new rules to the ILF in 1993, restricting its use to those under 66 with extensive care packages. The success of the ILF has continued to face subsequent governments with the dilemma of needing to prevent spiralling costs yet unable to ignore the fund's popularity with disabled people. Again in May 2010, the ILF rules changed, preventing access to the fund for any disabled person working less than 16 hours (Department of Work and Pensions, 2010). In December, 2010 the ILF was permanently closed to all new applicants. In April 2013, the government launched its Transfer Review Programme, which will see a final closure of ILF by April 2015. At this date, the funding will be devolved to local authorities in England who will have sole responsibility for meeting eligible care and support needs.

By the late 1980s disabled people, however, having had a taste of directing their own support, became more determined to bring about more permanent legislative changes to the system which would allow direct payments to become a viable option for those eligible for services. The British Council for Disabled People was a key player in the campaign for direct payments and actively lobbied members of Parliament for their support in changing legislation (Leece and Bornat, 2006), particularly targeting the emerging Community Care legislation. Some local authorities started to experiment with different forms of payment schemes known as indirect payments, either via a voluntary organisation or via a trust fund. A nervous Conservative government reacted by explicitly stating in the guidance of the 1990 NHS and Community Care Act that current legislation prohibited the making of cash payments in place of arranging services (DH, 1990), much to the disappointment of the Disabled People's Movement, which then went on to increase pressure for specific legislation in this area.

The 1990s

The year 1990 saw the introduction of the NHS and Community Care Act (implemented in 1993) with a focus on market forces and the belief that support could be tailored to individual need if the concept of consumerism was embedded within the provision of social care. At the same time social service departments came under increasing pressure to tighten criteria and to target scarce resources to those with the greatest needs (Glasby and Littlechild, 2009). In reality there was a growing consensus that the focus of intervention was being pushed further towards crisis management with less space for promoting choice and independence.

The Independent Living Movement continued to lobby members of Parliament. This determined approach, along with a timely piece of research carried out by Zarb and Nadesh (1994), provided the extra push needed for a Conservative government dwindling in popularity to change direction. The government, which could not deny the accordance of principles underlying direct payments with their own neoliberal social and economic policies, was persuaded in 1994 to change legislation and make cash payments available to disabled people with effect from 1996 in the form of the Community Care (Direct Payments) Act 1996.

RESEARCH SUMMARY

Research carried out by Zarb and Nadesh (1994), **Cashing in on independence?**, *remains a key piece of research in understanding the then Conservative government's decision to introduce legislation to enable cash payments to be made to individuals with an assessed need.*

Seventy disabled people in England using direct or indirect payments to purchase their support were interviewed. The study found that:

- *It gave disabled people a greater degree of choice and control and higher levels of user satisfaction.*
- *Support arrangements funded through payment options were more likely to be reliable (and therefore more efficient) than directly provided services.*
- *More cost-efficient support arrangements financed by direct/indirect payments were found to be between 30 and 40 per cent cheaper than equivalent service-based support.*

COMMENT

While all three key findings may well have influenced the Conservative government, the attraction of providing services/support at a cheaper cost is likely to have played a significant role in finally persuading the government to legalise cash payments.

Inclusion movement and person-centred planning

The Independent Living Movement, led primarily by physically disabled adults, clearly focused on extending choice and control to give disabled people the opportunity to live more independent lives. At the same time, similar ideas were emerging in the learning disability arena. Theories of normalisation (Wolfensberger, 1972) and social role valorisation (Wolfensberger, 1983) linked to ordinary life principles had begun to influence policy development and service delivery. This work influenced ideas around person-centred thinking which John O'Brien brought to the UK, proposing that work with people with learning disabilities should be informed by the *five accomplishments of community presence; relationships; choice; competence and respect* (O'Brien, in Brown and Benson, 1992). Supported by professionals and user-led organisations, individuals and their families began to embrace this approach and build pressure and demand for services and support to be developed in this way. This has often been referred to as the 'inclusion movement' and was very popular as long-stay institutions closed down and people with learning disabilities returned to their communities as part of the resettlement programme in line with community care policies (DH, 1989). Since this time, person-centred practice (PCP) has been developed in this country by key supporters such as Helen Sanderson and Peter Kinsella. Described as a *process of continual listening, and learning: focused on what is important to someone now, and for the future* (Sanderson, 2000, p. 2), PCP has influenced the development of the personalisation agenda both in terms of its relevance to practice but more importantly its fundamental principles of sharing power and community inclusion (Sanderson, 2000). An understanding and appreciation of the convergence of the Independent Living Movement and the Inclusion Movement is important in understanding the influence and impact it had on subsequent policy development.

1996 – Community Care (Direct Payments) Act 1996

First, it is important to remind ourselves that personalisation is not just about direct payments, personal or individual budgets. It is also important to recognise the impact that direct payments legislation had in shifting policy thinking in relation to service delivery and social care generally. The 1996 Community Care (Direct Payments) Act came into force on 1 April 1997. It was described by Oliver and Sapey (1999, p. 175) as having *the potential for the most fundamental reorganisation of welfare for half a century.* The Act gave local authorities the power (not the duty) to make payments to disabled people aged between 18 and 65. The local authority had to satisfy itself that recipients consented to receiving the services and understood the financial and legal implications they were undertaking, often referred to as being 'able and willing'. Since this original Act in 1996 a number of changes have been made to extend the use of direct payments in terms of both those eligible and the breadth of how the payment can be used.

In 2000, new regulations extended the age limit for recipients of direct payments to include people aged 65 and over in England. Similarly, the Carers and Disabled Children Act 2000 extended the use of direct payments to carers, parents and carers of disabled children and disabled children aged 16 and 17.

Perhaps the clearest signal that the then Labour government intended to widen the use of direct payments came in 2001 with the introduction of the Health and Social Care Act. Under Section 57 of this Act, local authorities are required to offer direct payments to all eligible individuals (those with an assessed need under S47 of the NHS and Community Care Act 1990 and who consent to and are able to manage the payments with or without assistance).

At first, take-up for direct payments was slow and patchy across the country and the government recognised that significant changes were required (Glasby and Littlechild, 2009). As a result, new guidance was produced in 2003 (DH, 2003a) identifying key changes including the relaxing of rules around the employment of close relatives, allowing consideration of long-term benefits in assessing cost efficiency and the injection of a £9 million Direct Payments Development Fund (DPDF) in 2003 to pay voluntary organisations, in partnership with local authorities, to set up additional information and support services.

In addition, direct payments became one of the Social Services Performance Assessment Framework indicators (DH, 2003b), signalling a serious commitment to widening their use.

Finally, it is important to note the change of government in 1997. Labour came into power with a new perspective which became known as the Third Way, combining the free-market ideas of neoliberalism with notions of responsibility, along with an emphasis on independence and choice (Clarke, 2004). The White Paper *Modernising social services* (DH, 1998) identified the key priorities as promoting independence, improving consistency and providing convenient, user-centred services. In this sense the direction towards direct payments and personalised services became politically attractive to the key political parties.

Moving into the twenty-first century

Building on some of the key thinking around person-centred planning and the lack of strategic direction for learning disabilities services since the early 1970s, the publication of the White Paper *Valuing people: A new strategy for learning disability for the 21st century* in 2001 set out 11 objectives aimed at improving the lives of people with a learning disability. Based on four key principles of rights, choice, independence and inclusion, in many ways this White Paper is reflected in much of the thinking and practice later articulated as 'personalisation'. For example, person-centred planning was first formally adopted as government policy in this White Paper. It has since been included as a key method for delivering the personalisation objectives of the UK government's Putting People First programme for social care (DH, 2008a).

ACTIVITY 1.3

Obtain a copy of the Valuing people White Paper (DH, 2001), which can be found on the Department of Health website www.dh.gov.uk. You will find that this White Paper set out 11 objectives. Look carefully at objective 3: Enabling people to have more control over their own lives. Identify three ways in which people with learning disabilities can be supported to gain more control over their own lives.

COMMENT

As you develop your understanding of the personalisation agenda and self-directed support, it will be interesting to note the links with your three answers above. Sometimes service users and professionals find it difficult to identify how services or support could help individuals gain more control over their lives because they are so used to traditional services such as day centres, respite care facilities, etc. As you will see in the following chapters, service users describe how some very creative yet simple solutions have led to them gaining more control. The case study below is one example of this.

CASE STUDY

Sally is a 24-year-old woman with mental health difficulties. She was unable to leave her home due to severe panic attacks. Sally lives alone and has no family and few friends to support her. She depended on daily visits from support workers to help her with personal care needs and to escort her to the shops, etc. Sally became very depressed as she wanted to have more time outside the house but depended on support. One of the support workers introduced Sally to her dog, which was a real success. Sally felt more relaxed around the dog and decided she would like to own her own dog to help her with her anxiety problems. Sally's social worker helped her complete a self-assessment and access an individual budget which she used to purchase a dog and to pay for dog food and dog training lessons. Six months later Sally goes out every day. She meets other dog walkers in the park and her anxiety levels have reduced dramatically. She now receives a weekly visit from support workers rather than daily visits. Sally says that Jesse (her dog) has helped her get her life back and she no longer has to depend on others.

The term 'personalisation' was starting to emerge as a frequent term in government circulars and White Papers. In 2005 a joint report by the Department for Work and Pensions

(DWP), Department of Health and Department for Education and Skills was published: *Improving the life chances of disabled people* (Prime Minister's Strategy Unit, 2005). In this report, the government recognised the benefit of personalising support through direct payments and committed to further research and development of individual budgets. Similarly in 2005, the DWP set out its strategy for supporting older people to achieve *active independence, quality* and *choice* in the services they receive in its report *Opportunity age* (DWP, 2005) and in 2006, the health White Paper, *Our health, our care, our say: A new direction for community services* (DH, 2006) described a *radical and sustained* shift in the way services were to be delivered. A commitment to ensuring that services were more personalised, whereby individuals had a stronger voice and became major drivers of service improvement, suggested that the government was about to embrace the notions of *deeper personalisation* that Leadbeater (2004) described in his new script for public services.

The White Paper of 2006 set targets to increase the use of direct payments and to develop and widen the extent of individual budgets whereby a variety of funds would be brought together. Individuals eligible would be offered a transparent sum which they may choose to take as cash or as a service or a mixture of the two, but with a common aim that it should offer them greater choice and flexibility (DH, 2006).

The ideas behind this White Paper in relation to individual budgets were heavily influenced by the work of In Control, a project set up in 2003 in order to find new ways of organising the social care system. In Control began to develop a model of working which promoted the concept of self-directed support, which led to the creation of the first individual budget. In Control began to offer support and advice to the government and local authorities around the idea and practice of individual budgets and self-directed support. In Control continues to be a key player in the development of self-directed support and it is worth spending some time accessing the resources on their website www.in-control.org.uk.

2007 and beyond

At the beginning of this chapter our journey started with the ministerial concordat, *Putting people first: A shared vision and commitment to the transformation of adult social care* (HM Government, 2007). In this document, the government set out four key areas in which individuals and communities may need support to ensure better quality services and choice and control in their lives. These areas are:

- universal services;
- early intervention and prevention;
- self-directed support;
- social capital.

Universal services
This refers to services that are important in everyone's lives to participate fully in their community. It refers not only to those people with care and support needs but provides a more inclusive approach to service delivery.

CASE STUDY

Joan is a 75-year-old widow living in rural area with little social interaction. She is healthy and fit and until recently has been able to drive to visit friends and local groups. Since she has stopped driving she has become very isolated. There is a limited bus service and she has a considerable walk to the nearest bus stop. A local co-operative has developed a volunteer car project whereby journeys can be booked flexibly by individuals who pay a basic reasonable mileage cost. It is being used widely within this rural community, making it more cost-efficient and bringing the individual cost down for all those using the project. Joan's life has improved significantly since the development of this scheme.

Early intervention and prevention

The second area refers to support available to assist people who need a little more help, at any stage in life, to stay independent for as long as possible. This may include help to safely maintain a home or training to get a job or return to work after a break.

CASE STUDY

As part of a Return to Work strategy, a local council provides a mobile careers advice service which involves a bus visiting local areas. Residents can easily access the support and receive advice on career choices, completing application forms or making free phone calls to local employers. The mobile service is aimed at encouraging people who may be more reluctant to pay transport costs to get to a more central service or find it difficult due to illness or caring responsibilities.

Self-directed support

This means having services available to meet people's needs rather than people having to fit in with the things on offer. It is about people who need support being able to choose who provides that support, and control when and where the services/support are provided.

CASE STUDY

Yusuf is a 19-year-old man with mental health problems. He lives at home with his mum, dad and two sisters. Yusuf has been offered weekly supported sports sessions at a local sports centre with a group of disabled people of a similar age. Yusuf has attended once and although he really enjoys sport he refused to return as he struggled with the amount of people and noise. Yusuf has now joined his personal budget with that of one other member whom he particularly likes. Between the two young men, they have enough money to employ a personal assistant to support them fortnightly with a sports activity which they choose alternately. The two young men have become good friends and are spending more time with each other outside this session.

Social capital

The fourth area of *Putting people first* is about society working to make sure everyone has the opportunity to be part of the community and experience friendships and care. It is about people becoming full members of the community. Social capital refers to engaging with people and showing them how they can influence the decisions that affect their lives.

CASE STUDY

A group of parents of adults with learning disabilities came together to work with the council to put ideas into practice to develop a telephone support line to support other parents in a similar position. The local council supported the group to grow through its own networks. The group has now developed a telephone support line which is operated by volunteers on a rotating basis which is manageable for all volunteers. The group of volunteers has now developed a social circle from this activity which has promoted their own health and well-being. The council fund this highly valued telephone support project and are responding to feedback at both a practice and strategic level in relation to future service delivery and developments.

Putting people first asserts that transformation of adult social care programmes should be co-produced, co-developed and co-evaluated and recognises that real change will only be achieved through the participation of users and carers at every stage (HM Government, 2007, p. 1). The example above is evidence of how parents and carers can be involved positively in each aspect of co-production from design, to implementation and evaluation. Research on co-production suggests that frontline workers should focus on people's abilities rather than seeing them as problems (Boyle et al., 2006) so they are empowered to co-produce their own solutions to the difficulties that they are best placed to know about. The telephone support line is a good example of capitalising on strengths and skills rather than problematising a vocal group of parents who are trying to improve the system.

ACTIVITY 1.4

*Visit **http://webarchive.nationalarchives.gov.uk**. and search for 'Putting People First – the whole story'. Read the two-page document and write one sentence to sum up your understanding of the four areas of focus:*

- *universal services;*
- *early intervention and prevention;*
- *choice and control;*
- *social capital.*

In pairs try to think of examples of how you might incorporate these four areas into your practice.

COMMENT

It is very important to think of personalisation in its broadest sense. Personal budgets have often been at the forefront of our minds when we think about personalisation but if we are to adopt the true essence of personalisation we need to think further than our work with individuals and consider how the community and society can contribute. It is only by thinking in this wider framework that we are likely to change our attitudes to welfare. Within a personalisation context this is essential if we are to shift the fundamental relationship between the state and the individual. If we can start to see individuals and communities as being capable of contributing in this way, we are more likely to place a higher value on their input and abilities.

The Social Work Task Force

In 2009 a report by the Social Work Task Force, *Building a safe confident future* (DH, 2009a), made proposals for the reform of social work over the next ten years including: the establishment of an independent National College of Social Work; an improved system of professional development, and a Licence to Practise for social workers. Leece and Leece (2011) suggest that the recommendations pose a contradiction to the personalisation agenda. On the one hand, concepts of personalisation and co-production are driving towards increased power and autonomy for individuals using services. The proposals contained within *Building a safe confident future,* on the other hand, intend to elevate social work to a new level of professionalism with a possible extension of power. It will be interesting to note whether these two agendas can coexist. The personalisation agenda calls for social workers to shift power over to service users in key stages of the process, including assessment, support planning and review. At the same time the safeguarding of vulnerable people is a key priority for the government as signalled by the Social Work Task Force (DH, 2009a). This in turn is likely to lead to increased regulation and social work presence in the lives of vulnerable people. Managers and social workers may struggle to make sense of these two policy contexts, which appear to be travelling in opposite directions.

ACTIVITY **1.5**

Obtain a copy of the 2009 Social Work Task Force report, which you will find at http://webarchive.nationalarchives.gov.uk. Read the executive summary of the report.

- *What do you think the key tensions will be for you as a social worker in supporting individuals to lead autonomous lives while ensuring you are being a responsible, accountable social worker?*
- *How might you deal with these tensions?*

(Continued)

(Continued)

COMMENT

Reading this report summary may have highlighted some of the tensions for you as a prac-titioner. As a social worker you will frequently come across situations where you have to balance your role as an enabler with one of protector. Within a personalisation context this can be even more challenging, especially given the current political climate in relation to the safeguarding of vulnerable children and adults.

2010 – A new administration, another new vision for social care

The Coalition government continues to reinforce a policy context which embraces personalisation, viewing it as central to social care improvement. The 2010 Local Authority Circular, *A vision for adult social care* (DH, 2010c), provided some clear messages that personalised services with clear outcomes will be expected in deliv-ering social care in the future. Armed with slogans such as 'Big Society' and 'Think Local Act Personal' (TLAP), government ministers clearly indicated that personalisation would be a central feature of an ongoing agenda for the public sector. This can be seen as evident in their support for the development of managed budgets, Individual Service Funds and Right to Control Trailblazer sites, the latter led by the Office for Dis-ability Issues (ODI) which tested out how disabled people can exercise greater choice and control over the following funding streams; adult social care, Supporting People, Work Choice, Access to Work, ILF and Disabled Facilities Grants. Following the evalua-tion of this project that was piloted in seven Trailblazer areas in England, the govern-ment is now considering how this might be rolled out on a wider basis (ODI, 2009).

The success of personalisation at an individual level has also been used to inform the broader public services agenda. The Coalition government has rolled out Community Fund Holding, introducing the idea of local authorities pooling budgets and com-munities designing solutions, determining outcomes and having greater control over spending as a means of increasing local choice and control, while delivering the stra-tegic and preventative outcomes commissioners require (Waters, 2011). Emerging research and interest relating to the notion of co-production has provided convincing evidence that we should centrally involve people who use services along with their carers and those at the front line of practice in the design and implementation of ser-vices and support models (Slay, 2011; TLAP, 2011). In both projects the authors urge us to rethink the capacity and assets that social and health care services utilise, in particular the knowledge, skills and experience of those who use services, their carers and front-line practitioners. This, they argue, requires a genuine shift from an empha-sis of treating people who are supported as passive consumers, based on a deficit approach, to one that provides opportunities to recognise and grow people's capa-bilities and actively supports them to put these to use at an individual and community level. Embedding notions of reciprocity, mutuality and blurring distinctions between those who provide services and those who receive services in this way can lead to wider perceptual transformations in that individuals feel valued and responsible in their roles and therefore have greater incentive to contribute. At a cultural level, perceptions and images of service users and vulnerable people in the eyes of the public may start to shift towards seeing people as active citizens having a positive contribution to make at both community and societal level.

The development of personalisation in the form of personal health budgets has accelerated considerably in the last few years. The personal health budget programme launched by the Department of Health in 2009 has reported positively on its first evaluation in 2012 including findings from 64 pilot sites. As a result of this evaluation, along with positive findings from the second national personal budget survey, covering over 3,000 people, 300 of whom were in receipt of a personal health budget, published by the TLAP partnership (Hatton et al., 2013), the government has committed the NHS to rolling out personal health budgets across England. By March 2014 all clinical commissioning groups will need to be able to offer personal health budgets to people receiving NHS Continuing Health Care, and by March 2015 everyone who can benefit will have the option of a personal health budget. A key challenge to making personal health budgets work for individuals requires strategic, cultural, funding and individual integration and co-operation. Social Care Institute of Excellence (SCIE)/Kings Fund (2011) found that divisions between health and social care make little sense to people using services. They expect joined-up services that give them choice and control. Furthermore, the adoption of a person-centred approach, which aspires to people experiencing one system of care and treatment, not several disconnected ones, is essential.

The developments highlighted above within both social care and health care appear to have been taken seriously by the current government. The Health and Social Care Act 2012 sets out clear obligations for the health system and its relationship with care and support, based on recognising integration across the NHS, public health and social care as the key means to achieving this. Likewise the Draft Care and Support Bill (2012), which at the time of writing was at the second reading stage in the House of Lords as the Care Bill, sets out a number of measures which, if accepted, will strengthen personalisation as the core to future service delivery within adult social care. Some of the key changes relating to personalisation that are likely to be secured within the subsequent legislation include:

- national eligibility criteria;
- legal entitlement to personal budgets to both adults needing care and their carers;
- portable assessment.

In addition the Act itself is set to embed a statutory principle that refers to people having real choice and control over their care and support.

The timeline in this chapter has provided an overview of the historical, economic, social and political contexts that have shaped and influenced the development of the personalisation agenda. As demographics change, with increasing numbers of people living longer with more complex conditions such as dementia and chronic illness, current forms of welfare will also need to respond and change. By 2022, 20 per cent of the English population will be over 65. By 2027, the number of 85-year-olds will have increased by 60 per cent (HM Government, 2007). It is only as this agenda unfolds and evolves that we will be able to judge whether notions of self-determination and independent living can be embraced and adhered to in the process of transformation. Faced with finite resources and economic global downturn, there is a huge challenge to *build on best practice and replace paternalistic, reactive care of variable quality with a mainstream system focused on prevention, early intervention, enablement, and high quality personally tailored service*, as described in *Putting people first* (HM Government, 2007, p. 3).

CHAPTER SUMMARY

This chapter has traced the history of social work and social welfare. When we study history we often look at important figures, groups, ideas and movements. We also need to be aware, however, of the process of history and think about how these events link together. Learning about history in this way helps us to understand why things are the way they are in the present and what might happen in the future.

It is important to understand the history of social welfare and the various influences that have led to personalisation as we know it today. The convergence of the independent and inclusive movements along with the need for governments to prepare for the demographic changes in the twenty-first century help us to understand why and how ideas get taken forward at the time they do.

While most human beings would agree that we should never return to the draconian methods of incarcerating the poor in workhouses, as happened in the early nineteenth century, the impact of such historical events for individuals currently dependent on state welfare and support is a constant genuine reminder of why concepts of citizenship, individual control and autonomy must remain at the heart of social policy. Disabled people have been campaigning for many years for changes in policy which allow them to have more choice and control, yet it appears that those demands have only been acknowledged and responded to once the potential fiscal benefits of such a change can be realised. It is hard to imagine that some level of cost–benefit analysis is applied in developing social care policies. It would, however, be naive to think that changes in government direction occur only as a result of governments developing their understanding of the 'best' or 'fairest' way to treat people. The truth is it is probably a combination of both. In relation to personalisation, we have seen that many different drivers with varied priorities have managed to meet in the middle and may have found, at least in principle, a mutually acceptable way forward in the form of personalising services and support. It is only as we look back in history that we will be able to judge whether a system of personalisation contained the key ingredients required to deliver high-quality, individually tailored support at a cost acceptable to the public purse.

Englander, D (1998) *Poverty and the poor law reform in 19th century Britain, 1834–1914: From Chadwick to Booth.* Essex: Longman.

This book provides students with an opportunity to consider early developments of social work and social welfare as far back as 1834. It demonstrates the links between early nineteenth-century welfare provision to the development of modern-day social welfare. The book is accessible and interesting, bringing together history, policy, legislation and practice.

Needham, C (2011) *Personalising public services: Understanding the personalisation narrative.* Bristol: Policy Press.

At the centre of Needham's argument is the idea that the personalisation of public services has been told and established as a 'policy story'. Thus, as the personalisation narrative has taken hold in policy circles, the major determinant of its success has been the stories and tales told about reform, as opposed to the research, evidence and impact of the policies themselves. The book offers a very accessible, thoughtful and nuanced analysis of personalisation.

Powell, M and Hewitt, M (2002) *Welfare state and welfare change.* Buckingham: Open University Press.

The book provides a clear account of the nature of the contemporary welfare state and explores how and why the welfare state has changed in Britain throughout history. In this book Powell and Hewitt have explored the ideas and argument which have been advanced to explain the process of change. The book will enable students to appreciate and understand the broader context of policy and practice.

www.scie.org.uk

An e-learning resource relating to personalisation can be found on this website providing more information in relation to history and current developments and practice.

www.thinklocalactpersonal.org.uk

Think Local Act Personal (TLAP) is a national, cross-sector leadership partnership focused on driving forward work with personalisation and community-based social care. It focuses on bringing together people who use services and family carers with central and local government, major providers from the private, third and voluntary sector, and other key groups.

Chapter 2

Personalisation – A value base for practice

Ali Gardner

Introduction

Personalisation is both a way of thinking and a way of doing. It cannot be viewed solely as a new system which social workers need to learn to operate. It must be understood at a more fundamental level which acknowledges the complex relationships social work and social welfare provision have with those who are in receipt of services. The importance of values in social work has long been accepted. There is increasing consensus that skills and knowledge are only a part of the process and that the way we filter information, make sense of it and use it to inform our actions is largely determined by our values. As Mullender and Ward (1991) state, *there is no such thing as value-free work, only workers who have not stopped to think what their values are.*

The underlying philosophy and principles guiding personalisation such as self-determination, dignity and choice must be fully understood by practitioners if they are to enable meaningful opportunities for individuals to direct their own support. We might assume that such familiar terms automatically inform the work of practitioners given that social work is committed to the following five basic values: human dignity and worth, social justice, service to humanity, integrity and competence (BASW, 2002). This somewhat dangerous assumption, however, ignores the complex factors impacting on our understanding and interpretation of these values.

In this sense social work values are never straightforward. They may change according to a situation; for example, a social worker's primary aim to care through supporting good parenting may quickly change to one of protection whereby actions have to be taken to remove a child or control a situation. Values may change over time whereby new research, understanding and debate influence change in policy or practice. Even within the relatively short time since the introduction of BASW's five basic values in 2002, social work landscapes have changed considerably. Influenced by serious case reviews and a rapidly changing political and economic context, our understanding and expectations of the social work role and process have shifted considerably. Today we are seeing increased pressure for social workers to assert more power in their role in relation to child protection following the death of Victoria Climbié in 2000 and Baby P in 2007. Similarly, depleting resources and changing demographics can influence notions of need. While social work may be fundamentally influenced and committed to certain core values, external influences such as those mentioned above will determine the extent to which these values can be realised and embedded within social work practice. In this sense values themselves cannot always be taken as absolutes.

One final influence on our values is public perception. Social work has increasingly found itself in the media spotlight, attracting public debate about how services should be funded, organised and implemented. Clearly, interest in the delivery of services which are publicly funded is a valid part of a democratic society and highly influential on the social care task. The collective beliefs about the 'right way' to provide for people's needs become embedded within societal perceptions and in turn inform the value base of social work.

ACTIVITY 2.1

Try to find a recent newspaper article or news report in relation to social work. This might be a child protection case, a report on asylum and immigration, an attack on a member of the public by a person with mental health problems, or local authorities allowing people to buy a football season ticket with their personal budget.

(Continued)

(Continued)

Here is one idea to get you started.

An article from the Manchester Evening News, *17 December 2007.*

NHS pays for season ticket

A SICK football fan was given NHS cash to buy a season ticket for a fellow supporter to keep him company at home matches.

This was the headline in a local paper referring to a man who used his individual budget to pay for his personal assistant to accompany him to football games. Without this support the service user would not be able to attend the football matches which had been a significant and valuable aspect of his social life prior to his disability. See if you can find similar headlines by searching the internet or maybe you can remember some that have appeared over time.

Discuss the issue with a partner and try to list the values underlying this report. Think about some of the following points.

- *Was the report positive or negative?*
- *Who was at fault or blame?*
- *Do you think your family or friends or the wider community would share a similar view?*

COMMENT

Reporting of social work-related issues is often presented in a way to evoke emotion and to encourage the reader to question the rights and wrongs of the case, particularly in the tabloid press. The public response to such articles affects the social work task in many ways. It gives government a sense of public opinion which may in part lead to legislative or policy changes. It also affects the people whom the articles are written about. In Chapter 5 service users provide us with an insight into public perception about their personal budget and the pressure it can put on them.

Values

One of the interesting features of our values is that we tend to adopt them unknowingly and stop recognising them as a key part of our practice. Thompson (2005, p. 11) suggests that *we tend to become so accustomed to our values and beliefs that we do not recognize that they are there or how they are influencing us. An important step, then, is to be clear about what our values are.*

In order to help us consider our value base in relation to the personalisation context, we will consider the concepts:

- paternalism;

- citizenship;

- social and medical models;

- partnership;

- anti-discriminatory practice;

- use of self in practice;

- critical practice;

- empowerment.

But first we will take time to complete a short exercise that will inform our thinking in this chapter.

ACTIVITY 2.2

- *On your own make a list of as many words as you can associated with the word 'client'.*
- *Now make a list of as many words as you can associated with the term 'citizen/ citizenship'.*

If you are working with someone, share the lists and discuss the words you have associated with each term. Think about the following.

- *Did you use positive or negative words?*
- *Did you struggle to find words associated with either term?*
- *Have you ever been a client? If so, how did it feel?*
- *Do you or have you ever perceived yourself as a citizen? If so how did it feel?*

COMMENT

We will return to these words and their meaning later in the chapter but it will be useful to keep a note of your responses and see if your reading leads to you thinking about these concepts differently.

Paternalism

As discussed in Chapter 1, the development of the welfare state in 1948 paved the way for improved social and health care for many people in the UK. Embedded within this model of care was the assumption that the state would decide what and how to provide services to people in need. This saw the emergence of a paternalistic or 'nanny' state in which individuals in need relied on the expertise of the professionals to assess and provide the appropriate service.

The following quotation, taken from Minister Douglas Jay in 1937, illustrates the thinking of this time.

> *In the case of nutrition and health, just as in the case of education, the gentle-man in Whitehall really does know better what is good for the people than the people know themselves.*

(Jay, 1937, p. 317)

Personalisation rejects this paternalistic approach to social care and prefers to see the individual as better placed to make decisions about how their needs can be met. This change in direction, however, is no easy task for policy-makers, managers, social workers and providers. Deeply embedded paternalistic values developed throughout their training and rooted within their practice can make this a challenging shift. Social workers may need to examine their relationships with service users and realign their values, skills and practice in viewing people as experts in their own right rather than passive recipients of care. As Smale et al. (1993) suggest, changing practice requires workers to change the assumptions they make about individuals. This discussion then leads us to question the contribution or added value of social work. What expertise, if any, can social work offer in the process of assessment and service provision? In Chapter 3, we will explore this issue in more depth, where it will be argued that while social workers' roles may need to adjust in the way they relate to and support service users, they do have a key role to offer in relation to enabling, navigating, advocating and promoting the rights and needs of service users.

Citizenship

What does it mean to be a citizen? In the exercise above you were asked to think about words you associated with 'citizen'. You might have suggested rights, entitle-ments, social inclusion, and liberty, among others. Marshall and Bottomore (1987) have widely contributed to our understanding of citizenship in a modern society. In their work, Marshall and Bottomore trace the development of citizenship, noting the significance of the end of the Poor Laws. Marshall and Bottomore define citizenship as a *status bestowed on those who are full members of a community. All who possess the status are equal with respect to their rights and duties with which the status is endowed* (p. 18). Prior to 1918, those relying on poor relief in reality forfeited their civil rights of personal liberty by internment in the workhouse. This stigma, however, of depending on government support has been difficult to shake off and perhaps explains why notions of citizenship have continued to remain an aspiration rather than a reality for those in need of support. The sticking point is that service users continue to be seen essentially as having needs rather than being supported to exer-cise their rights. To be a citizen means having social rights and being included within society. Thompson (2005, p. 124) claims that *social work practice plays a pivotal role promoting or underpinning the citizenship status of particular individuals, families or groups who are otherwise prone to social exclusion.*

The Disabled People's Movement has been influential in promoting notions of citi-zenship, pointing out that disabled people's rights are often neglected as a result of social workers' focus on providing care services rather than on supporting the right to be able to participate in society (Oliver and Sapey, 1999). Duffy (2004, p. 9) claims:

today's human services have been built around the professional gift model of service delivery, which assumes that needy individuals will be given what they need by the professional who understands those needs.

Duffy (2006) describes the 'professional gift model' as being characterised by the *person in need* at the bottom of the chain relying on the professional to provide a service which has been funded by the government via taxation by the community. In this sense the person in need is more prone to be perceived by others and potentially themselves as *needy, reliant, tragic,* or *different* and grateful for the care or service that has been given. This reflects a paternalistic approach.

In contrast, Duffy (2003) describes the 'citizenship model' as promoting notions of rights and entitlements in the way agencies and professionals relate to individuals. The person is central to this process rather than simply being a recipient of care. The model recognises the individual engaging with their community at different levels, including: accessing support and services; choosing and directing support; making use of community activities and facilities and importantly contributing to that community. Duffy (2003) suggests that no one in society defines their life or their ambitions simply in terms of receiving social care. Duffy urges us to start thinking about the *keys to citizenship*: self-determination, direction, support, money, home, community life. While challenging social exclusion is fundamental in promoting and achieving citizenship, it also requires service users to be supported to actively contribute as citizens within their communities. In Chapter 3, we will explore the ways in which social work can support this process through self-assessment and support planning focusing on the keys to citizenship as defined by Duffy.

Our understanding of citizenship and its importance within a personalisation context is two-fold. First, our engagement with service users requires us to support social inclusion and, second, in challenging processes and attitudes which perpetuate marginalisation, stigmatisation and social exclusion. Not only is it important for an individual to feel like a citizen, they must be treated as a citizen too. In Marshall's analysis, cited in Thomas et al. (1992), he referred to citizenship being *bestowed* on individuals, suggesting the importance of individuals being recognised and thus treated as citizens with equal rights. As described earlier, there is increased public and media interest and judgement in relation to who should and who should not receive welfare and on how that money should be spent, and arguably both can be linked to the concept of 'bestowing citizenship'.

It may be straightforward for society to understand and accept that public money can be used to pay for disabled people to live in a residential placement as they cannot look after themselves in their own home or attend a day centre which offers daily activities and companionship. It is perhaps not as easy for society to accept that someone may choose to take driving lessons to meet a social care need even if this happens to guarantee the best outcome.

Understandably there is public interest in how well the money has been spent. Unlike other evaluations of services, there is a somewhat curious approach to judging whether money has been spent wisely in social care. A satisfied taxpayer will often perceive value for money in social care if a disempowered, tragic and needy person is the result. This appears to reinforce the view that there was in fact a genuine need. It appears more difficult to perceive money as being well spent if the result is a healthy, empowered individual functioning well in society. One respondent in Henwood and Hudson's study (2007) commented, *we don't worry about all the money we waste on crap institutional provision, but we worry about giving someone £20.*

CASE STUDY

Phil is a 66-year-old man who lives alone, having recently lost his partner. Phil has a long history of mental health difficulties and always relied on his partner Tom to escort him when socialising outside the home. Phil's mental health significantly declined after the death of his partner of 20 years. Phil has not been out of the house much and relies on friends coming to the home for any social interaction. His social worker told him of a local drop-in, which he might benefit from, but Phil said this just wasn't for him. With some help from his social worker, Phil was able to identify his need to socialise with others outside the home to reduce his isolation. He was also able to identify bowling as one activity he had enjoyed with Tom. Phil was supported to get a small personal budget which he used to pay for a set of bowls and for a friend to support him for a month to enable him to feel comfortable getting to the bowling club and socialising with others. After four months Phil feels able to travel independently to the club. He has joined a team and plays weekly games. He is still reserved but does talk to a few members who are very supportive. Phil still has episodes of ill health but bowling is something he feels able to return to as soon as he is feeling in better health.

COMMENT

Judgements relating to value for money in social care appear to have somewhat different criteria compared with other public services. If extra money is given to a failing school which then improves its performance and achieves better results, we view this as money well spent. If social care money is spent on individuals leading more independent 'normal' lives whereby they can engage in ordinary, inclusive social, leisure, education and employment activities, it can often be assumed that the money was not actually needed in the first place and was not well spent.

Personalisation is not immune to public debate surrounding the 'deserving' and 'undeserving' and what society will tolerate and sanction. It is important, therefore, that social workers understand the complex conceptualisations involved in promoting choice and control at an individual level while promoting notions of citizenship by challenging social exclusion at a structural level.

RESEARCH SUMMARY

A national study, Here to stay? (Henwood and Hudson, 2007), used in-depth qualitative case studies to provide a detailed understanding of progress with self-directed support implementation. The study took place across three localities in the UK, at different stages of implementation. The sample included senior policy staff, commissioners, care managers, elected members and chief executives. It looked at ways in which people understood personalisation and their judgements about the desirability and feasibility of implementa-tion. The study highlighted a variety of conceptualisations and judgements and found no ideological consensus in relation to self-directed support. Interestingly the study identified a number of ideological obstacles.

- *The 'giving and doing' tradition – social workers do as much as they can for the service users and secure for them the most support possible.*
- *The loss of collectivism – evidence of a tension between the emphasis on the individual rather than the collective objectives.*
- *The conflation of needs and wants – a view that personalisation addresses people's extravagant wants rather than their needs.*
- *Mistrust of service users – evidence of explicit and implicit suspicion that people will seek to get as much out of a system as they can, while the professional has a responsi-bility to protect the demands on public funds.*

The quotations below reflect some of the thinking so far in this chapter.

How do you stop yourself doing a needs assessment when you have been doing it for ten mil-lion years? I don't think people can just shift the skills they have always used that are embed-ded and valued.

(Head of service)

A lot of elected members are resistant to losing control and not providing services. It's very much about what we do as paternalistic and it's hard to change.

(Lead member)

I am not anti and I am not signed up to the cult. I am somewhere in the middle. I want to be really dynamic but also measured, controlled and safe.

(Care manager)

I just thought this is for me. It was potentially earth shattering in that it could significantly change the power balance between the state and the individual. It was a huge moment for me.

(Senior manager)

Social and medical models

It is worth noting the links between paternalism and citizenship in relation to the social and medical models of disability. The medical model has tended to focus on

27

the physical limitations of the individual and views diagnosis as a starting point to dealing with illness and disability. The importance of understanding the cause of someone's illness or disability provides the key to work towards a cure, control or management. While some researchers, such as Watson (2003, cited in Grant et al., 2005), claim merits in the medical model approach, the last 20 years have seen the emergence of a new paradigm for understanding disability: the social model.

The social model of disability emphasises the physical and attitudinal barriers that exclude a disabled person from participating fully in society (Oliver, 1990). Essentially the social model views disability as something society imposes upon a person. It acknowledges that while some people may have physical, sensory, intellectual or psychological variations, these impairments do not have to lead to a disability unless society fails to take account of these and adapt to ensure inclusion.

Both the medical and social models have been criticised for presenting somewhat simplistic views of their position in relation to disability (Barnes and Mercer, 2010). The complex nature of disability and impairment has been well documented and this debate cannot be covered fully in this text. It is important, however, to recognise a growing voice in disability politics which suggests that both the personal experience of impairment and the social exclusion imposed by a disabling society need to be acknowledged and integrated in a full analysis if we are to understand and respond to how disability and impairment operate. For many years the suppression of the subjective experience of impairment has been intentional in forcing governments and society to acknowledge the disabling barriers it creates. Crow, in Barnes and Mercer (2010), asserts that if all disabling barriers were removed, some people with impairments would still face disadvantage, for example limitations to an individual's health or their experiences of pain may constrain their participation in activities. Crow goes on to suggest that we need to acknowledge the experience of impairment, without underplaying the overwhelming scale of disability and that only then will we be able to achieve a route for change.

REFLECTION POINT

The professional gift model described above could be seen to reinforce medical model thinking in that the person is viewed as needy and that professional support will help manage the problem. In contrast, the citizenship model focuses on including the individual in directing support which can enable inclusion.

ACTIVITY 2.3

To illustrate the importance of underlying values in the way we perceive individuals, read the following information.

Omar is a 25-year-old disabled man who cannot meet any of his personal needs. He needs 24-hour support and will need two people to support him outside the home. He has challenging behaviour and becomes very aggressive if he doesn't get his own way. Omar uses no verbal communication and relies on others to interpret his needs.

Think about this extract of information. What picture do we have of Omar? What do we know about him? Reflecting on the chapter so far, answer the following.

- *Does this information reflect the medical or social model? (Discuss your answer in pairs. Think about how and why you have chosen the model.)*
- *Does this information describe a client or a citizen? (Discuss the difference with reference to the professional gift model and citizenship model.)*

COMMENT

Hopefully you spotted that this information reinforces the medical model. It sees the problem resting with Omar. There is a negative focus on his needs and it fails to recognise that the environment or the way he is supported contributes to his disability.

ACTIVITY 2.4

Thinking about Omar using the social model, try to write a paragraph to describe his situation. Try to present Omar as a citizen.

COMMENT

As social workers we sometimes forget to include service users' strengths as we focus on the problem or the weakness that has been identified in the referral. Sometimes the systems we work within can persuade or force us to adopt a medical model approach in order to access and secure services for service users. Social workers are always aware of the financial constraints they are working with and that resources are targeted at those deemed as most needy. It is important, however, to highlight and maximise service users' strengths and expertise wherever possible.

The introduction of government guidance, the Fair Access to Care Services framework (FACS) (DH, 2003c), set out to address inconsistencies across the country in relation to who gets support, in order to provide a fairer and more transparent system for the allocation of social care systems. It could be argued, however, that such inflexible screening and assessment systems, while attempting to standardise practice and offer transparency, leave little space for service users to be described within their own personal contexts in an inclusive manner. Henwood and Hudson (2008) suggest there is an inherent tension between FACS and the personalisation agenda in that:

> *the latter is based around self assessment, self determination, choice and individually geared support focused on a wide definition of health and well being.*

> *The former is reliant on tightly circumscribed categorisation, standardisation,*
> *consistency of treatment and explicit decision-making.*

There has been some government recognition of the shortcomings of FACS in relation to personalisation with the introduction of government guidance seeking to
deliver a whole-system approach to eligibility (DH, 2010b). While it goes some way
to acknowledging local community needs as well as individual needs, it still requires
social workers to operate within rigid boundaries in deciding whether they have an
eligible need and therefore become entitled to a resource.

There lies a complex maze of tensions for social workers to navigate. On the one
hand, they have to work within a medical model framework which dictates criteria
and allows little flexibility yet may lead to more resources. On the other hand, they
are aware of the need to adopt a social model approach in which they should value
and highlight the strengths and uniqueness of each person. The tensions between the
social and medical models are not new to social work but the personalisation agenda
does challenge this analysis further. This process is worthy of reflection as the model
the practitioner adopts will inform their conceptualisation of the professional task.

To illustrate this we shall return to the example of Omar above. It is clear to see how
our understanding and conceptualisation of this scenario influences the professional task. If we perceive Omar solely as a disabled person dependent on others to
think and act for him, then our actions are also likely to reflect this perception. In
our assessment our primary focus will be Omar's needs. In turn we are more likely
to adopt a paternalistic approach in which we rely on our own expertise and professionalism to design a care plan that best meets his needs. In this sense we have
understood Omar's situation and reacted to his situation within a medical model
framework. If, however, we believe that there is more to Omar than the case notes
suggest, we are likely to adopt a social model approach and try to understand why he
is behaving in an aggressive manner and consider more creative ways of communicating with him to find out his wishes. In practice, an integration of both the medical
and social models is required. The social worker understands the impairment while
working to minimise or remove factors which disable the service user and limit their
opportunities to participate and direct their own support.

Partnership working

So far we have tried to unravel some of the underlying values and theories influencing
our practice as social workers. We now need to consider how we engage with service users, their families and other stakeholders in supporting individuals to direct their
own support. The answer may appear simple: *we work in partnership*, and it is certainly easy to say we do this; but what does it actually mean to work in partnership?

Partnership between service users and professionals has long been established as a
core component of social work practice. Legislation and government guidance have
promoted the concept of partnership working in all aspects of social work from community care to child protection. Marsh and Fisher (1992) propose that the principles
upon which partnership is practised include: user agreement, involvement, negotiated

agreement, and users having the greatest possible choice of the service offered. Pugh and De'Ath (1989, cited in Braye and Preston-Shoot, 2001) suggest partnership can be understood as a continuum from involvement in a decision through to the service user being in control of the process.

At its simplest level partnership working means working with service users and other agencies, rather than doing things for them, and this is a good starting point. Thompson (2006, p. 123), however, suggests that it requires:

> ...*a degree of humility to accept that professionals do not have all the answers and clients have a major contribution to make in resolving the difficulties that have been identified.*

Although this quotation precedes the development of self-directed support, in many ways it captures the essence of personalisation. It steers social workers away from adopting the professional gift model and working within a paternalistic framework. Instead it recognises service users as having insight into their own needs. It views them as citizens with relationships and connections within families, networks and communities which only they fully understand. Many solutions and sometimes support can be found within these networks but the social worker must take the lead from the service user in unlocking this understanding.

The mandate for partnership working was introduced formally in the NHS and Community Care Act 1990 with an emphasis on consumer power. It was assumed that the inevitable outcome of the Act would be the ability of service users to express their choice and act upon it. Armed with clear guidance in relation to decision-making procedures, channels of complaint and involvement in assessment and planning, service users would be able to assert their own views on how best to meet their needs. While these conditions went some way to changing the working relationship between the service user and the professional, the absence of one key ingredient – cash – meant that true consumerism could never be achieved.

Arguably, Community Care failed to reject a paternalistic approach to social work with adults. As a result, the somewhat tame gestures of handing over power and control remained largely tokenistic. The framework and terminology, which at its time may have appeared radical and refreshing, actually only served to reinforce the belief that power remained securely with the social worker and the state. At second glance, however, shouldn't we have seen the writing on the wall? The clues may have been in the language used to describe this process: *care management, care manager* suggesting the need for someone to be in charge of care. At one level, care management claimed to be about *tailoring services to individual needs* yet at another level social workers were required to act as *gate keepers, secure service* and *support and control the delivery of the care plan. The role of the practitioner is to assist the user in making choices from these resources, and put together an individual care plan* (DH, 1991). The language used within care management suggests the values underpinning this process were based on a paternalistic model whereby the 'expert' care manager/social worker would support the service user to make 'sensible' decisions about how best to meet needs. One has to question how far we have journeyed from the sentiments of Minister Jay in 1937 in claiming that the gentleman in Whitehall really does know better what is good for the people than the people know themselves (Jay, 1937) – in reality, perhaps only as far as the gentleman in the town hall.

In contrast, the development of the personalisation agenda is based on a more radical form of partnership working which insists that power is transferred to the service user in relation to assessment, support planning and crucially the allocation of resources, the money. Its success is based on a model of citizenship which places the individual at the centre and encourages professionals and service users alike to work together in identifying natural, community and paid support rather than thinking purely in terms of services.

Finally, a word of caution in understanding partnership working. It would be naive to believe that intention alone will enable us to develop equal partnerships with service users. This assumption ignores the powerful structures and processes inherent within local authorities and society at large. Social workers must always acknowledge the power they hold in each interaction with a service user. No matter how much control we transfer to service users, the gatekeeping role of the social worker has not been removed. Social workers hold significant power at each point of the process whether it be access to resources or reviewing the outcome. Service users will be ever aware of this relationship and the risk it carries in terms of accessing or keeping a resource. The service users we will hear from in Chapter 5 clearly illustrate this point.

Anti-discriminatory and anti-oppressive practice

If we acknowledge the central role of power in both our relationships and the professional task of social work, we must also learn to recognise its presence and seek to reduce its impact wherever possible. In practice, power can be seen to operate at a personal and structural level. The status afforded to individuals is often something deeply embedded within our consciousness before we have even met an individual and will be informed by a range of factors including race, gender, class, etc. As social workers we often enter situations bringing a power which we may not even recognise. In addition, power can be derived through perceived threat; for example, a service user may perceive a visit from a social worker as intrinsically linked to imposing some control in their lives. Finally, structural power is ever present in that social workers often enter situations with a mandate potentially affording them powers to take controlling measures in a given situation. In this sense, social workers have considerable access to power over service users. Social workers must seek to make sure that they not only recognise discrimination and oppression in the lives of service users but ensure their own practice does not add to or exacerbate their oppression.

Social workers play a pivotal role between the state and its citizens. Every intervention can lead to either potential empowerment or potential oppression (Thompson, 2006). An understanding of anti-discriminatory practice and anti-oppressive practice is therefore essential. The difference between these two concepts has been a constant focus of debate. Thompson (2006, p. 13), claims the difference to be *primarily semantic rather than theoretical and ideological*, while others including Braye and Preston-Shoot (2001) resist these terms being used interchangeably. Braye and Preston-Shoot suggest that anti-discriminatory practice is *reformist, challenging unfairness or inequity in how services are delivered, whereas anti-oppressive practice is more radical, seeking a fundamental change in power relationships* (p. 54).

In relation to personalisation, I would suggest that distinguishing between the two is important. In this context, anti-discriminatory practice is concerned with how we engage with service users and their families, designing processes which promote equality, widening access to resources, along with some of the basic prerequisites such as treating people with dignity and respect and promoting self-determination. Personalisation, however, requires a more radical approach to working with individuals, as we have seen above. Social workers need to develop an acute understanding of structural inequalities. They need an awareness of oppressive legal structures and practices and an appreciation of the histories and relationships that exist between those in receipt of services and those responsible for providing welfare. Only then will social workers fully appreciate the need to realign power relationships at a more fundamental level in order for them to be seen and treated as citizens able to lead change in their own lives. In this sense anti-oppressive practice is more concerned with challenging social constructs of need based only within a paternalistic model. It relies upon an alternative conceptualisation of individuals with rights and entitlements located within a citizenship model of thinking and practice.

An important feature of anti-oppressive practice is a requirement for social workers to be proactive in their work with service users. They must adopt a questioning approach and be willing to question underpinning knowledge and values informing policy, guidance and practice. Social workers in this sense see more than descriptions of individuals and their scenarios; they understand and analyse this information by locating it within wider social, geographical and political contexts. Social work then becomes a dynamic process whereby social workers develop creative ways of working. Burke and Harrison (2007, cited in Adams et al., 2009) suggest that these ways of working, informed by a complex, critical, politicised and geographical view of our culturally plural society, will contribute to the development of relevant and appropriate services.

ACTIVITY 2.5

This exercise will help you to develop your understanding of anti-discriminatory and anti-oppressive practice.

The Direct Payments Act 1996 states that all individuals with an assessed community care need are entitled to and should be offered the option of receiving a direct payment.

- *Consider the responses of the social workers A and B.*

Social worker A

'Yes, Mr Walker, you have been assessed as having a community care need. You have two choices. You are entitled to a direct payment. This will be money given to you for

(Continued)

(Continued)

you to spend as you choose. You will be responsible for employing someone and dealing with the money. It is quite a difficult process and a lot of older people find it very hard. Personally I don't agree with them but you can have one if you want. The other option is I could sort out some home care to come to you twice a day to help you to get out of bed in the morning and back in at night.'

Social worker B

'Yes, Mr Walker, you have been assessed as having a community care need. It's really important that we work together to make sure you get the right support. I can tell you about your options so you can make the right choice for yourself. You are entitled to a direct payment. This is a system whereby the local authority will give you money so you can choose how to spend it. You can choose whether to employ an agency or a personal assistant perhaps. You can have support to help you with this process and I could ask someone from our local direct payments team to come and talk to you if this would help. I can leave this leaflet with you today which gives you examples of how other people have used direct payments. You may prefer to use our home care service to help you in the mornings and the evenings. I can organise this for you if you choose this option. It might be useful to have some time to think about it, read the leaflet and discuss it with your family. Have you any questions at this stage? I will come back in two days so we can talk again.'

Now think about the difference between the two approaches by answering the following questions.

- *Identify examples of anti-discriminatory practice.*
- *Identify examples of anti-oppressive practice.*
- *Can you identify any values underpinning the practice of social worker A?*
- *Can you identify any values underpinning the practice of social worker B?*

COMMENT

Hopefully the exercise illustrated the importance of both anti-discriminatory practice and anti-oppressive practice as well as the difference. Social worker A probably fails to adopt either an anti-discriminatory approach or an anti-oppressive approach. While she does inform Mr Walker of his entitlement to a direct payment, she does not provide him with any information or confidence to take this option. Her connection with Mr Walker is based on the professional gift model, in that she is the expert, she knows what he needs and she can sort these out. In short, she tells Mr Walker what is going to happen. She also appears to be unaware of the power she holds in this exchange.

Social worker B, on the other hand, provides a fuller picture in relation to direct payments. First, she clearly tells Mr Walker about his entitlements. She provides him with additional information and gives him time to digest information and discuss it with his family. She appears to value Mr Walker's contribution and underlying this short exchange

> *social worker B demonstrates respect and promotes self-determination. There is also an indication that she is aware of wider social and political contexts and the power she holds as a social worker. She gives Mr Walker time to consider his position, for him to reflect on the information. In doing so she is offering meaningful potential for him to make an informed decision and lead the way in directing his own support. At the same time she reassures him that she will support him to make the right decision. In this brief exchange we return to the words of Thompson (2006). Every intervention can lead to either potential empowerment or potential oppression.*

Self and practice

It would be an impossible task to do social work without connecting in some way to the values and principles that underpin practice. While many jobs require the ability to analyse and interpret information, social work requires a personal engagement at a deeper level. Morgan (2012) provides a useful framework for supporting students to access new ways of thinking which are essential for transformative practice to occur. In her work, she makes a distinction between *core concepts*, the building blocks of a subject that need to be understood to enable the progressive understanding of that subject and *threshold concepts* which lead to new ways of thinking that have previously been inaccessible. The notion of *threshold concepts* emerged in the early 2000s from the work of Meyer and Land (2003) when they described a threshold as a *portal* to a new understanding of a subject.

In her work, Morgan refers to the five central characteristics of a threshold concept being: transformative, irreversible, integrative, bounded, and troublesome. She uses the example of understanding the *social model of disability* to illustrate the shift students make when they begin to unravel many of their preconceived ideas about disabled people as tragic, passive individuals in need of professional support. Through immersing themselves in new knowledge and looking through new lenses they begin to see the external factors and barriers constructed by society as being responsible for disabling individuals rather than the problem being located within the individual. Morgan suggests that this process allows the student to pass through the *threshold* and this in turn allows them to practise differently. Morgan describes the need for students to *get it* and that once they have *got it*, i.e. passed through the threshold, the significant shift in perception gives them access to new knowledge and new ways of thinking about things. In this sense the process is irreversible. Once an individual has passed through the threshold it is difficult to step back or understand why one could have ever thought in that way. For students it can also be difficult to understand why other students can't *get it*, as it now somehow appears so obvious. Meyer and Land (2003) note the integrative nature of threshold concepts in that they expose the previously hidden inter-relatedness of something and that this, in turn, allows individuals to make new connections which were previously hidden to them.

Finally, this process can be very troublesome for students as they move away from previously deeply held beliefs that have, in part, formed their identity and ontological assumptions about the world. Many students can also find this an alienating process as they manage this transition and begin to experience a growing distance from peers, family or friends who have not shared this journey. In relation to personalisation, the student needs to pass through a threshold whereby they can genuinely value and respect the individual as the person in control with the expertise. As Morgan suggests, this is a troublesome time as we relinquish our dependence on professional expertise and instead seek to engage in meaningful partnerships with service users. Within a personalisation context, passing through this threshold leads us to new ways of thinking and working with individuals. Importantly the fundamental shift in thinking, which essentially becomes a different way of being, makes it less likely that we will slip into old habits of controlling and deciding for service users. Instead the starting point comes from the individual and the social worker adapting their skills to become an enabler and facilitator rather than a manager of services and support.

The use of self in practice is almost inescapable. At times most social workers would probably like to take a break from the constant questioning and professional and personal dilemmas they are faced with. This is made all the more difficult as assessments, decisions and interventions can lead to significant changes or consequences in another individual's life. We only have to think about the dilemmas social workers face in deciding whether a child is at 'significant risk of harm' or whether a person with mental health problems should be compulsorily detained. The ability to understand, interpret, analyse, consolidate, reflect and review information is central to the role of a good social work practitioner.

REFLECTION POINT

To help you think about the use of self in social work practice, consider the following analogy.

Reg has just started a car mechanic apprenticeship. On day one the boss gives Reg his own toolkit and tells him how each tool works and when it should be used. By the end of his training he assures Reg that he will know all the tools well and will be able to make decisions about when to use them. He will also be shown how to make sure all his tools are in good and safe working order.

Social work students might be given some basic information about the course on day one such as a timetable and an assessment schedule. They will also have to fill in lots of forms and probably pay out more money for various registrations, but what about a toolkit? Social work students will quickly come to realise that they already have a toolkit – a virtual toolkit, the self. In the same way as the car mechanic, Reg, the social worker will need to learn about the toolkit and the individual tools. In order to use the tools effectively, social work students will also absorb knowledge and experience as part of the course. Once new information or an experience is taken in, trainee social workers will start to use their interpreting tools. The knowledge they have recently acquired is only part of the picture as our personal values informed by our biographies, past experiences and cultural norms begin to filter what is seen, begin to make sense of it and evaluate its worth. As we saw at the beginning of the chapter, Mullender and Ward (1991) suggested that there is no such thing as value-free practice.

The acceptance of the self in practice is the key starting point for all social work students. Braye and Preston-Shoot (2001) suggest that the ability to learn, unlearn and relearn is vital to social care practice. The ability to recognise when and how we connect with new information and knowledge is fundamental in beginning to fine-tune our tools so we are ready for practice. As a social work student on your first home visit or as a practitioner, you might imagine your virtual toolkit: remember to check that your tools have been well conditioned before your visit and make sure you don't leave them in the back of the car!

Critical practice

If we acknowledge that knowledge, skills, experience and values play a significant part in social work practice, we need to make sure that we continually monitor and self-regulate our thoughts, beliefs, decisions and actions. Jones (2013) states the importance of students being reflective and reflexive within their practice. Students must learn to analyse professional activity during or after an event. Jones goes on to suggest that students should use supervision or discussions with colleagues to gain a deeper understanding of an experience which in turn will improve practice. Schön (1986) describes reflection as being both in-action (i.e. when we are immersed in a situation) and on-action (i.e. after the event when we can rewind situations and be more retrospective). In addition to being reflective, social workers need to adopt a reflexive approach to their practice. Reflexivity is different from reflection as it involves challenging and critiquing oneself at a broader level. Jones (2013, p.106) claims that reflexive practice *causes us to evaluate our position within our practice from a personal involvement perspective*. Webb (2006, p.107, cited in Jones, 2013) provides a more radical definition of reflexivity:

> *A reflexive practitioner is engaged in radical confrontation with the very ethical basis and legitimation of practice and self involvement, introducing an important moral dimension into social work that is lacking in the reflective practice literature.*

In relation to personalisation, I would suggest that the more radical activity of reflexivity is essential. Throughout this chapter we have explored the importance of realigning fundamental social work values in order to see people as experts in their own lives. Practitioners must recognise and examine the complex relationships social work and social welfare have had with those in receipt of services. It is only by critically drawing on the histories and biographies of marginalised groups that we can fully appreciate and develop new ways of working with service users based on this new paradigm. For example, the history of personalisation needs to include an understanding of the position of disabled people and the emergence of the Disabled People's Movement. The campaigns based on the insistence by disabled people to be treated as citizens with rights and entitlements are central to a self-directed model of support. Clearly it is important that practitioners reflect on their practice and continually analyse the professional task and their relationships with service users. However, the ability to be reflexive and challenge not only oneself but the ethical basis of practice (Webb, 2006, cited in Jones, 2013) is more likely to lead to a longer-lasting commitment to the core principles underlying professional practice.

Empowerment

The term 'empowerment' is familiar to all practitioners, but do we ever give enough time to think about what it means? We might suggest that empowerment is about giving power back to service users or enabling people to make decisions or take actions to improve their lives. This is part of the process, but unless we recognise that it is about more than facilitating or enabling people to do things then it is unlikely that the changes individuals make will have a long-lasting effect or benefit to their life. This type of support may, perhaps, help people to function better in their day-to-day life, or improve their interpersonal relationships. Professionals, however, must encourage service users to understand the connections between their own circumstances and the broader sociopolitical context in which they exist. Professionals and service users must take seriously the significance of disadvantage and oppression that service users face in everyday life. It is a matter of connecting the personal with the political and from a service user perspective, using this insight to motivate oneself to make decisions and changes which are likely to have a lasting effect. The belief of the necessity to take an action becomes more important than the ability to take the action as the individual develops an internal compass which can navigate them through complex situations and decisions. Service users begin to take control of their lives and work in a way which alters existing power relations between themselves and professionals or agencies rather than working within them. This radical rather than functionalist approach to problem-solving is based on a combination of cognitive and emotional factors which is more likely to equip service users with the confidence and skills to demand services and support based on what they want rather than what is imposed upon them.

Empowerment must be at the core of personalisation. Professionals must see this emancipatory value as their focus of practice. Glasby and Littlechild (2009) claim that research and evidence relating to direct payments and personal budgets so far provide the most powerful tools available for increasing choice and control available to disabled people and for changing the relationship between the state and the individual. Many service users have never been given the opportunity to engage with services in this way and it is not something that will necessarily come naturally to them. It is not as simple as handing over power. It will take time and support for individuals to take the driving seat in this process and develop their skills along the way. Personalisation reinforces the idea that the individual is best placed to know what they need and how those needs can best be met. It assumes that people can be responsible and make their own decisions but people need the information and support to do so. If we return to Activity 2.5 and think about the responses of the two social workers, we can see that social worker A in the brief exchange makes assumptions about Mr Walker's abilities and wishes. She allows her own values to dominate the exchange and makes it clear that if he does choose to go against her advice, he will be doing so alone, clearly reinforcing where the power lies. In scenario B, the social worker assumes Mr Walker is capable of making a choice, she identifies that he may need more support and offers it in the form of leaflets and readings about how others have used direct payments. She makes it clear that his choice will be respected and supported and in so doing hands over power to Mr Walker, laying down the foundations for empowerment.

One final word of caution in relation to empowerment and personalisation: social workers need to guard against casual claims and assumptions that they are functioning as empowering practitioners. Empowerment instead should be viewed as an aspirational rather than attainable value or goal. Assuming we have empowered people runs the risk of an unhealthy level of complacency creeping into our practice. As individuals begin to take control of certain aspects of their life they may well begin to transfer this experience and learning to other areas of their life. When individuals make the link between the personal and political, they begin to acquire the confidence to open further opportunities to develop, liberate and transform. The role of the social worker is to ensure that information and support are offered to individuals, to carefully judge the level of support and encouragement individuals need and more importantly to know when to withdraw.

CHAPTER SUMMARY

This chapter has explored the complex relationships between those in receipt of services and those providing services. It has considered how they have emerged, and are reinforced or challenged by past, present and future government policy, ideologies, theories and models of practice. Central to the discussion is the importance of adopting anti-discriminatory and anti-oppressive practice which seeks to support service users in making connections between personal circumstances and political structures. Good partnership working based on reflective and reflexive practice provides the means to hand over control to service users in a way that they feel comfortable with and confident to make meaningful changes to their lives.

Advocates of personalisation have described it as a new paradigm while the more cynical view is that it is little more than a cost-cutting exercise. In reality both perspectives have probably influenced the agenda. I would suggest that personalisation has the potential to be embraced as a new paradigm if practice is based on a comprehensive understanding of the concepts discussed in this chapter. Social care professionals need to understand why it is important to give people power before they learn how to do this. Students need to be supported by educators to pass through the threshold concept as described by Morgan (2012) and really get it to enable them to practise differently. In this sense, empowering practice in personalisation is about both thinking and doing.

FURTHER READING

Duffy, S (2006) *Keys to citizenship: A guide to getting good support for people with learning disabilities* (2nd edn). Birkenhead: Paradigm.

An excellent explanation of citizenship and how it can be achieved in practice.

Glasby, J and Littlechild, R (2009) *Direct payments and personal budgets. Putting personalization into practice* (2nd edn). Bristol: Policy Press.

This book reflects on the history of direct payment and the personalisation agenda. It refers to a range of research in relation to different service user groups and provides useful analysis throughout.

Henwood, M and Hudson, B (2007) *Here to stay? Self-directed support: Aspiration and implementation (a review for the Department of Health)*. Heathencote: Melanie Henwood Associates.

A very accessible piece of research providing insight into how professionals are responding to the personalisation agenda.

Jones, S (2013) *Critical learning for social work students.* Learning Matters: Exeter.

This is a most accessible book helping students to develop their skills in critical thinking and using self in practice.

Morgan, H (2012) The social model of disability as a threshold concept: troublesome knowledge and liminal spaces in social work education. *Social Work Education: The International Journal*, 31 (2): 215–26.

This is a very interesting conceptual journal article which supports students to understand and articulate the personal journey they may pass through in social work training

Oliver, M and Sapey, B (2006) *Social work with disabled people* (3rd edn). Basingstoke: Palgrave Macmillan.

This book encourages students to critically reflect on practice and provides a good level of detail of the social model of disability both for those new to the concept and those with some grounding. The book explores the links between the social model of disability and direct payments legislation and policy and considers how far this legislation has promoted independent living principles and empowerment.

WEBSITES

www.in-control.org.uk

In Control started work in 2003 to change the social care system in England and committed to individuals being in control of their support and lives. The website has a wealth of information relating to policy, practice and experience from people directing their own support.

www.york.ac.uk/inst/spru/

Social Policy Research Unit, York University (SPRU). Their work has been concerned with the development of policies and the delivery of services to support people made vulnerable by poverty, ageing, disability or chronic illness. SPRU has an international reputation for excellence in research. There are several studies and useful articles relating to personalisation.

www.thinklocalactpersonal.org.uk

Think Local Act Personal (TLAP) has an area dedicated to personalisation and provides more details of the policies and reviews mentioned in this chapter.

Chapter 3

Personalisation in practice

David Gaylard

Introduction

This chapter critically examines the current context of personalisation in practice. Applied research findings will be linked throughout the chapter. The key processes involved in self-directed support will be outlined before concluding with the challenges that extending the personalisation agenda presents during a period of austerity.

Personalisation is perhaps the most significant change to the delivery of services by social workers since the NHS and Community Care Act 1990. Community Care legislation at the time was seen as ground-breaking in that it looked at trying to meet the needs of people in need in the community as opposed to resorting to institutionalisation as the first recourse (Burton et al., 2012).

The language of personalisation

Before exploring the process of self-directed support, it is important to point out that there are several terms currently being used to describe services and modes of delivery within the personalisation agenda. It is worth noting that as with all new concepts, practice and terminology can evolve and change. Some of the terms are often used interchangeably and vary depending on the organisation or local authority you are working with. So at this point it would be useful to take some time to study the Glossary (located at the back of the book) to become familiar with the terms used throughout this text.

Why personalisation?

There is insufficient space to fully explore in critical depth the historical origins of personalisation, which has been explored elsewhere (e.g. Glasby and Littlechild, 2009; Burton et al., 2012; Gray and Birrell, 2013). However, a brief contextual overview is imperative to aid your understanding of the changes personalisation has brought to social policy and practice.

Personalisation has its roots in the Disability Rights and Independent Living movement, which started in California in the 1960s, and has at its core the social model of disability. The origins of the Independent Living movement in the UK go back to the late 1970s. The first Direct Payments legislation was enacted in 1996 with practice guidance the following year. In 2003–05, In Control started to pilot Personal Budgets and Self-Directed Support, initially with 60 people with learning difficulties in six authorities (Poll et al., 2006).

This chapter reflects upon the key differences between the care management model of practice and the self-directed support model of personalisation. In order to fully understand the concepts behind this agenda we need to look at its emergence across the UK and outline what is meant by personalisation, as it is open to different interpretations and implementation across the UK.

Personalisation under devolution

Personalisation is a relatively recent term that has, in a short space of time, became the 'big idea' – the dominant ideology in current social policy which has attracted support from successive Westminster governments. Since devolution, the ideas associated with the concept of personalisation are found in social care policies in each of the four countries of the UK, but have been pursued more vigorously in England.

In Scotland, self-directed support has been used to encompass greater choice and independence on the part of users.

In Wales, a number of policy documents refer to a vision rooted in a social model of disability in a rights-based approach that promotes choice and equality. Significantly, under a heading of *Citizen centred services*, it suggests the Welsh approach would not follow the consumerist approach adopted in England, noting that

> the label of personalisation has become too closely associated with a market-led model of consumer choice but we are taken with the Commission's approach to stronger citizen control.

> (Welsh Assembly Government, 2011, para. 3.16)

In Northern Ireland, there are references to personalisation within a number of policy documents but no concrete policy or targets regarding broader approaches to personalisation.

From care management to personalisation

The NHS and Community Care Act 1990 promoted the care management model of social work intervention. A key aspect of care management was that the process of assessment should be based on the expressed needs and preferences of the service user (Parker, 2010). The key stages of the care management model (summarised in Figure 3.1) is a clearly laid out process which social workers followed with service users. The social worker was perceived as the professional 'expert' who assessed needs and devised a care package for those in need (subject to a resource allocation panel decision chaired by senior operational managers). Within this model, service users were seen as passive recipients of services who did not know how much money was being spent.

Care management model	Personalisation model (Self-directed support)
Assessment of need	Self-assessment
Resource allocation panel	Resource allocation system (RAS)
Care planning	Support planning
Implementation and monitoring care plan	Implementation of support plan
Periodic review of care plan	Review

Figure 3.1 Key stages of intervention

Adapted from Burton et al., 2012, p. 45

ACTIVITY **3.1**

Look at the two practice models summarised in Figure 3.1 and make some notes regarding the similarities and differences between the two approaches and processes involved.

(Continued)

(Continued)

COMMENT

You might assume that there are in fact very little differences between these two models above. Both models include an assessment, a process of identifying and arranging support and services, resource allocation systems and reviewing the support once it is in place. There is much shared language in these two approaches which appear to be rooted within self-deterministic principles. However, if one looks a little deeper at some of the language used to describe the tasks we can start to identify some of the subtle, yet significant, differences.

As outlined in Chapter 2, one of the key levers for individuals gaining more control of their support came with the introduction of direct payments. The freedom and flexibility that came along with having money in their own hands cannot be overestimated, both in terms of personal spending power but importantly the victory it represents for disabled people who campaigned for years for the right to control their own support in this way. The release of funds to the individual is certainly one of the most, if not the most, striking differences between these two models.

Traditionally, most services were designed in ways that required people to fit in with what was on offer – the one-size-fits-all approach – rather than the other way around. Instead of supporting people to be connected or reconnected to their own communities, people were brought into separate services that were considered to be the most appropriate way to meet their needs. Perversely, such services often indirectly resulted in the exclusion and isolation of people with the highest level of needs due to inadequate staffing ratios or geographical location of the service.

Despite its good early intentions, care management as a system for delivering support to people was at very best a limited success, and for many was perceived as a failure. This was because it was premised upon a largely managerial (budget-saving) model which suggested that people needing social care support could readily be served in the same way as can customers for train tickets: there is a bewildering array of tickets and fares, but the ticket clerk has the information to find people the best solution for their needs – or so it is claimed (Williams and Tyson, 2010).

Some authors (Williams and Tyson, 2010; Duffy 2007) claim that the community (care management) system also failed citizens in a second, more profound way: it neglected their deep concerns and interests, their strengths (or gifts), and by doing so alienated them, and sometimes in fact confined them to a version of *institutional care* which did nothing to encourage or nurture them, or indeed give them due respect or dignity, or to make the most of the contribution of those who loved and cared for them. Social workers were given the job of assessing needs and sourcing care and it is to their credit that many did this well, while others left the profession or rebelled in other ways. Care management developed as a process and a system and hence was ill-equipped to enhance practitioners' creativity and skill. An in-depth critique of care management can be found in *The McDonaldization of Social Work* (Dustin, 2007).

Arguably, what was required involved a significant cultural shift in the way which support is provided to individuals and the role of social work within that process. Therefore, the modernisation agenda in England has resulted in an increased emphasis on individualisation and on user-directed and controlled services.

The focus has increasingly been on changing the role of adult social care service users from passive recipients of services to active citizens (or managers) of their own support, as exemplified in the Green Paper *Independence, well-being and choice* (DH, 2005) and *Our health, our care, our say* (DH, 2006). Focusing on needs and outcomes for individuals and their carers by working in partnership to promote choice and control is an undoubtedly positive development, particularly when one considers the argument that traditional social work (or least some aspects of it) had somewhat lost its way.

Personalisation and Fair Access to Care Services

Fair Access to Care Services (FACS), originally introduced in 2002 (with revised guidance published in 2010, DH, 2002, 2010a), provides national eligibility guidance that aims to prioritise and allocate resources to those assessed as being in highest need of social care support by providing a consistent approach that local authorities apply, helping address some of the inequalities, discrepancies or 'postcode lottery' criticisms in funding arrangements across the country.

It provides a national framework for allocating social care resources fairly, transparently and consistently. The eligibility framework is divided into four domains: *low*, *moderate*, *substantial* and *critical*, which are assessed in terms of the risk to an individual's independence as a result of a range of social care needs (summarised in Figure 3.2). Authorities are free to interpret the criteria in respect of the needs of their local budgetary community needs, so they set their own threshold for providing services and use of resources available but must take account of national guidance.

FACS does not require local authorities to provide services to everyone regardless of the banding that they are assessed within. The aim of FACS guidance is not to standardise services but to ensure *individuals with similar difficulties receive similar outcomes* (DH, 2002, p. 30) by providing a strategic framework that is applied, minimising inequalities that may occur due to different local authorities' approaches and resource allocation priorities (Bogg, 2012).

However, many local authorities increased their FACS (DH, 2002, 2010a) eligibility thresholds to critical and substantial domains only in terms of the risk of an individual's independence. This results in only those with the most complex highest needs receiving services. As a consequence, those with critical and substantial needs are often in chronic or acute, physical ill health and/or in a state of emotional crisis so may not be in a good position to make potentially long-term choices for co-ordinating their future care arrangements. Therefore, it has been claimed that from a purely eligibility perspective, most service users and carers who are in a position to be assessed as personalisation originally intended are now unfortunately screened out as moderate need (Gray and Birrell, 2013; Henwood and Hudson, 2008).

Critical: when

- Life is, or will be, threatened;
- Significant health problems have developed or will develop;
- Serious abuse or neglect has occurred or will occur;
- Inability to carry out vital personal care/ domestic routines;
- Vital involvement in work, education or learning cannot or will not be sustained;
- Vital social support systems and relationships cannot or will not be sustained;
- Vital family and other social roles and responsibilities cannot or will not be undertaken.

Substantial: when

- There is, or will be, only partial choice and control over the immediate environment;
- Abuse or neglect has occured or will occur;
- There is, or will be, an inability to carry out the majority of personal care or domestic routines;
- Involvement in many aspects of work, education or learning cannot or will not be sustained;
- The majority of social support systems and relationships cannot or will not be sustained;
- The majority of family and other social roles and responsibilities cannot or will not be undertaken.

Independence

Moderate: when

- There is, or will be, an inability to carry out several personal care or domestic routines;
- Involvement in several aspects of work, education or learning cannot or will not be sustained;
- Several social support systems and relationships cannot or will not be sustained;
- Several family and other social roles and responsibilities cannot or will not be undertaken.

Low: when

- There is, or will be, an inability to carry out one or two personal care or domestic routines;
- Involvement in one or two aspects of work, education or learning cannot or will not be sustained;
- One or two social support systems and relationships cannot or will not be sustained;
- One or two family and other social roles and responsibilities cannot or will not be undertaken.

Figure 3.2 Fair Access to Care Services eligibility bandings (DH, 2010a)

ACTIVITY **3.2**

Before undertaking any statutory assessment, ensure that you are familiar with the local authority's policies and procedures when applying FACS (some provide illustrative practice examples of key domains). Remember that FACS applies to the risk to independence, not simply risk of harm or other incidents. It is important to consider an individual's aspirations as the central elements of an FACS assessment if you are to appropriately apply the criteria.

- *Which bandings does your local authority provide services for?*
- *What are the local thresholds of eligibility in use?*
- *How might you provide a personalised approach to applying FACS?*
- *What good practice points might you need to consider?*

COMMENT

Remember that a person-centred assessment needs to consider the person within their social context, while promoting active participation and involvement often has a positive impact upon other FACS domains and an individual's overall well-being.

It is important to consider informal (community) support networks; if they are not appropriate, state why. Analyse your assessment to ensure you demonstrate how needs, aspirations and strengths interact. Choice and control remain key themes in a personalised approach so all your activities (from assessment of eligibility, support planning and reviews) should consider the user's and carer's involvement with a view to maximising choice and control.

The process of personalisation

We have seen that the process of self-directed support is distinctly different from the more traditional models of assessment and service delivery, as it aims to involve genuine partnership working between the local authority, citizen and the family and friends, and potentially, a range of providers from statutory, voluntary and private sectors.

The focus is on agreeing what needs require to be met; identifying the resource available to meet those needs; engaging in discussions as to how the resource can be used; and defining mutually agreed outcomes to be achieved with the use of those resources (MacKay and MacIntyre, 2011). We have seen in Figure 3.1 that there are several key stages involved in the self-directed support process.

Self-assessment

A key change to the self-directed support process is the notion of self-assessment, whereby greater emphasis is placed on service users identifying their own needs. For many years social workers have had the power through legislation to assess adults in need and to manage the process of service delivery. Disabled people have argued that they should be able to assess their own needs and have the power and control over service provision (Renshaw, 2008).

The starting point for any adult wishing to access statutory social care services is the NHS and Community Care Act 1990. Section 47 provides local authorities with a duty to offer an assessment to anyone who appears to have a social care need. This part of the process is carried out to make an initial assessment and FACS is applied to determine eligibility. Depending on the threshold of the individual local authority, there are a number of possible outcomes at this stage. It may result in a simple service, piece of equipment or one-off intervention. This can be picked up in the initial assessment and acted upon without requiring drawn-out assessment processes and long-term intervention. It may lead to signposting to other appropriate services, such as re-enablement, or prevention services. An initial assessment, however, may lead to the next level of assessment whereby a worker will be allocated and advice and information about the process are given to the individual.

As Morris (2004) highlights, independence is not linked to physical or intellectual capacity to care for oneself without assistance; it is about having control over that support and when and how that assistance is provided. This definition of independence remains centrally important in our understanding of self-directed support. A personalised approach, however, recognises that most people will be able to identify their own needs (as opposed to 'wants') although some may require more support than others to do this. This process of supported self-assessment does not replace a local authority's legal obligation but should properly form a key part of the assessment of need (MacKay and MacIntyre, 2011).

Several local authorities now use some form of a self-assessment questionnaire which the service user works through either alone or with a professional. Most questionnaires ask service users to score their needs against each question. At the end the points are added up and an overall score is given. The questionnaire asks a number of questions based on several domains covering all aspects of social care, for example personal care needs, nutritional needs, practical and daily living, physical and mental well-being, relationships and social inclusion, choice and control, risk, family carer and social support.

The depth and detail of the assessment must remain proportionate to an individual's needs, enabling more resources to be focused on those with complex needs. While it is important for practitioners to remain mindful of risk or potential risk, it is equally important in a self-assessment process to allow users to direct the process at the pace and sequence that they are comfortable with. This has often been challenging for social workers who may have traditionally worked within a more prescriptive care management model, where the professional lead and judgement remained central to the assessment process (such as the *professional gift model* – Duffy, 1996, 2006).

Developments in the self-assessment process and the self-directed model of support continue to raise a number of questions regarding the future role for social workers within this process. In general, the ways in which social workers can support service users include:

- Supporting service users to articulate and identify their own needs verbally and through written forms.

- Supporting people through major transitions often involves loss. Assessments frequently occur during times of significant upheaval or stress where individuals have to adjust to major transitions e.g. loss or bereavement, a new illness or disability.

- Supporting service users themselves to negotiate with members of their family, friends and carers who may hold differing (or opposing) perceptions, values, expectations or needs.

The tasks and roles mentioned above require specific expertise and skills which, it could be argued, lie at the heart of good practice. The introduction of self-assessment does raise questions about the future role of adult social work if service users are doing it for themselves. However, key skills are still required to facilitate service users to identify and articulate their own needs while supporting often fragile, sensitive situations and difficult relationships in order to sustain long-term positive outcomes. One of the common misconceptions of self-assessment is that it is a process that is exclusive to the service user. The aim of self-assessment, however,

is that service users fully participate in the process based on the pr
they are likely to be the best experts on themselves. The expertise
worker is therefore to advise, support and facilitate the service use
process, contributing their own expertise and experience in relatio.
cess. Unfortunately, post-qualified practitioners have since reported that tru,
encouraged to implement the entire process from a baseline of one home visit –
which was never how personalisation was originally piloted or recommended due
to workload process pressures.

Person-centred planning

In order to ensure that the service user is placed at the centre of each stage of the process from assessment through to support planning and review, social workers must adopt a person-centred approach to their work. Person-centred planning approaches seek to use what is important to the individual as the focus for developing support and change. This model of practice has been adopted as a key method for delivering the personalisation objectives in the Putting People First programme for social care (DH, 2008a).

The person-centred approach is very much reflected in the self-directed model of assessment (developed by In Control) whereby service users are encouraged to be centrally involved in this process from the start rather than it being a professionally driven document which at best might be shared with the service user on completion.

So it is important that practitioners see assessment as a shared process in which the service user has the skills and expertise to fully engage in the process. The skill of the social work practitioner is to help draw out that expertise so that service users can confidently express their own needs.

It is important to remember that many people who access services have been historically disempowered by dependency-creating welfare services, so may lack the confidence, knowledge or social capital to identify their needs or to make informed choices about the support they need (Priestley, 2004). In addition, they may not have the professional language to express their needs in ways which match process-driven assessment formats. So it is vital that social workers acknowledge this and support service users to identify their own needs. It is important to develop inclusive mechanisms and documentation that enables service users to articulate their needs in a way which makes sense to them rather than the wider organisation. It is important also to note the added value that local, user-led, independent charities such as the Independent Living Association can offer in supporting service users in the self-assessment process (Renshaw, 2008).

Within the assessment process it is important that the social worker encourages and enables people to make the best use of their own strengths, capabilities and resources to live independently. Thompson (2005) reminds social workers of the importance of focusing on strengths and avoiding the tendency to see themselves as problem-solvers who concentrate solely on weaknesses and see their role as fixing situations and providing expert advice.

Resource allocation system (RAS)

The social worker will then apply for the service user to meet the defined support needs through the resource allocation system (RAS, usually a points-based system). This system is operated by most local authorities and works out the financial resources to be allocated to an individual (deemed eligible for support) after an assessment has taken place. The formula used relates needs to points which equates to a cash value. Implementation of these arrangements is variable across the UK – in some parts it is still the main system in use, while in other authorities alternative RASs, are being contemplated – as there is no unified system within or across the UK.

Social workers complete the questionnaire answers in the assessment tool which generates the RAS, but it is sometimes regarded (by practitioners) as a tokenistic figure which creates a calculated indicative amount that often becomes the subject of a variation request to reflect the real cost of the service which may have already been proposed. Some practitioners now perceive the RAS as a 'care management' tool which is no longer fit for purpose.

Once the budget is identified the person is advised of the amount they have to 'spend'. The social work role then involves discussing how they wish to use the indicative resource to meet intended outcomes. This can be drawn as a direct payment, all or in part, allocated to a third party to manage on the person's behalf or left as a virtual budget where the person does not wish to exercise any direct control over the funding, for example a care managed budget.

Once an indicative amount has been identified, the council assesses the service user's financial circumstances in accordance with the guidance on *Fairer charging* (DH, 2003a). The council calculates what the service user's maximum contribution will be in accordance with *Fairer contributions guidance* (DH, 2010b).

However, practitioners continue to claim that by using an RAS to determine funds available is not really 'personalised' as needs have to be reduced to tick boxes that a computer system can calculate. There are several issues with this. As long as an assessment has been completed in a personalised way, the needs can be reduced to fit the boxes. The RAS generates an indicative amount that may not be accurate for all being assessed so should only be used as an indication of the amount of funds required. The decision as to the final amount available should not be made until after care planning and brokerage, as it is only then that you know if the amount is sufficient. If these processes are followed then it should be 'personalised' as each individual's needs and situation are taken into account.

Inevitable variations occur, with some social workers being informed that the RAS is the final amount with no additional funds available to future negotiations, resulting in a further variation to the RAS being granted to meet the needs of each individual. It continues to remain a contentious issue as local authorities are required to manage finite resources. So local authorities vary in how they apply the RAS, for example depending on the location where a service user may live – a rurally isolated or busy urban area – coupled with an individual manager's interpretation of budgetary constraints within the same locality. In 2009, Adult Directors of Social Services in association with In Control produced a *Common resource allocation framework* (ADASS, 2009) with the aim of addressing some of the technical, financial, legal and policy difficulties local authorities were experiencing in administering the current RAS system. It is hoped that the framework will enable a more standardised approach to be used in which everyone with similar needs and circumstances is treated equitably.

Power is where the money lies, so by giving service users the power over their own budget is the ultimate rung in the ladder of empowerment. This is not without its challenges of resistance from both social workers and service users who view this change with some scepticism (Burton et al., 2012). However, a source of tension within the self-directed process has been identified by social workers as the cut-off point following the assessment and allocation of funding stage. The stages of support, plan design and implementation are now likely to be picked up either by the service user with support for their family or by an unqualified support broker.

Support planning

Support planning is the means by which information is presented to a local authority in order to agree the release of funds as either an individual or a personal budget. The support plan highlights the lifestyle choices and wishes of the individual and demonstrates how the individual intends to spend the money to meet their aims. The support plan must be outcome-focused and reflect the needs identified in the self-assessment. The outcomes should be specific and indicate how they will improve the health and well-being of the individual and will keep them safe. A good support plan will also highlight any personal outcomes, which are things the person wants to achieve or change in life, as a direct result of being able to get the support that they need. The support planning process commences once the funds available have been agreed through the RAS process. At this point the social worker will make the user aware of the funds available and will discuss the support planning process. The social worker needs to provide information about what support planning entails and who might be able to help them with it. The key social work role is to enable planning to happen. For some this support may be minimal – it may simply involve providing basic information and signposting individuals to useful resources – while for others it could involve intensive support.

Duffy (2010) suggests that social work support should be focused on developing personalised support for the minority of people where no one else can provide the significant help they require. Duffy continues to reinforce the importance of equipping people to plan for themselves and to be in control. He suggests that social workers need to know how and when to intervene in the planning and implementation process – this is central to good practice. An ability to know when and how to offer an indirect and facilitative approach, which is more likely to have longer-term benefits and avoid creating dependency or incompetence from the service user's perspective, can sometimes be a challenging task for social workers.

Support planning is not a one-off activity and it is important that individuals are supported to continue to update and refine their support plan when necessary. The support plan may need to be updated as individuals achieve outcomes, or wish to change the outcome or support they receive. Ongoing support planning may be vital for those with rapidly changing or fluctuating conditions which impact upon their capacity to consent. In such cases there may be a need to continually refine the support plan to ensure that it meets a person's own priorities, needs and goals while ensuring that they are safe and that it is having a positive impact on their health and well-being. For those who lack the capacity to consent, it is important to ensure the support plan focuses on decision-making. In some cases it may be appropriate to set supported decision-making principles and agreements. Following the Mental Capacity Act 2005 Code of Practice, good practice in supported decision-making enables individuals to be supported to provide capacity to consent (DH, 2008b).

Finally, support plans need to be developed in a style that addresses risks in a proportionate flexible manner. It is important to ensure that the support plan explores issues of risk or potential risk and puts into place agreed safeguards (see Chapter 6). For some individuals, however, safeguarding mechanisms will not be necessary or appropriate and it is important that practitioners and organisations avoid employing a standardised or universal procedure that has to be completed for every individual. Some local authorities have introduced additional documents relating specifically to what could go wrong and how a person may manage this. Such documentation can then be adopted as an integral part of the support planning process if necessary.

The support plan needs to address key areas for it to be signed off by the local authority to release the funds. In Control (2007) developed the following seven criteria which should be addressed in order for this to happen. Many local authorities have adapted this model in establishing local support planning processes:

1. What is important to you?

2. What do you want to change or achieve?

3. How will you spend the money?

4. How will you use your individual budget?

5. How will your support be managed?

6. How will you stay in control of your life?

7. What are you going to do to make this plan happen?

The local authority needs to be satisfied that all the above questions have been addressed and that risk issues have been considered and appropriate safeguards put in place (if required) in order to agree the release of the funds. As with the self-assessment, the service user can choose how they will develop their support plan. They may decide to do it in one or more of the following ways.

- *On their own* Service users may choose to complete their support plan without any support. It is important to recognise the strengths and resources service users have in accessing and organising support. The internet and other technologies enable many service users to research and secure support and services which are specifically suited to helping them achieve outcomes.

- *Help from family or friends* Service users sometimes organise themselves into a trust called a 'trust circle'. This is a legal entity and can be very helpful to people who need support in making decisions or need *others to do so on their behalf.*

- *Service providers* Service users may already have positive relationships with existing independent service providers who already know a lot about them. The service user therefore may prefer to ask them to help develop the support plan.

- *Social workers* It is important that social workers see support planning as part of their role, providing this is the choice of the service user. In the past the initial assessment often dominated practice, sometimes paying less attention to other stages of the process such as care planning and reviewing. Glasby and Littlechild (2009) suggest that the self-directed support model has reversed the current practice and a focus on the support planning stage is a better place to start in ensuring the best possible support arrangements are put in place.

- *Independent organisations/support brokers* Some service users may choose to access support from someone outside their local authority, such as the Independent Living Association. It is likely that the service user will have to pay for this support but they can include this as part of the support plan. They may use different individuals or agencies to help them with different aspects of their plan. They may prefer to use a 'life coach' to help them think about changes, a technician to advise them on assistive technologies, or a financial adviser to help them work out the best use of the budget. Some of the independent agents include: independent advocates, direct payment support schemes, and independent person-centred planning facilitators, financial advisers or support brokers who carry out a range of tasks and functions to support the design, arrangement and management of the support plan.

ACTIVITY 3.3

Now that you have read about support planning, this activity will give you an opportunity to put it into practice. Case studies in relation to personalisation are useful as they help you to reflect on the creative ways people have organised their support. But this activity will help you think more creatively about support and enable you to help service users to think 'outside the box'.

You are the lucky winner of £1,000.

Your local authority has awarded you with this money to spend as you choose to improve your health and well-being. Here are the rules:

1. *You must spend it all within a year.*
2. *You cannot spend it on anything illegal or to pay off any debts.*

(Continued)

(Continued)

3. *You cannot give it away.*
4. *You must demonstrate the outcomes you will achieve for all the money, i.e. how will it improve your health and well-being?*

Your local authority will confirm whether or not your application has been successful. Use the box below to help you complete this task.

Amount £	Item/activity/task	Outcomes: How will it improve your health and well-being?

COMMENT

You may have found it relatively easy to think about how you would spend this money; but did you find it as simple to provide measurable outcomes which would improve your health and well-being? Could you try applying the FACS critical or substantial eligibility needs; if so, how did this limit your creative outcomes?

If you compare your own box with others in your group, you will note the diverse ways in which people spent their money, as we all have different priorities, responsibilities and networks of support. The importance of this activity is to demonstrate how diverse individuals are in identifying their needs and wishes.

If you had all been given a year's membership at a gym which you could only attend on Monday mornings, would this have suited the whole group? I hope you and fellow students employed some creative lateral thinking. Some of the examples previous students have suggested include: speed dating; meditation course at a Buddhist temple; horse riding, swimming or driving lessons; adult education classes; a cookery course; buying saucepans or a laptop.

The review

The review of self-directed support provides a real opportunity for the service user to reflect on their support plan. It is important that the principles of choice, flexibility and self-determination are embraced during the review phase.

Focusing upon the strengths and expertise of the service user, it is the social worker's role to support individuals to reflect on and review the outcomes that have been set as part of their support plan. Many authorities have adopted the term 'outcome focused' to describe this process which puts the main focus on the results being achieved for the person and their family. The outcomes identified in the support plan enable the service user and social worker to determine how well the support plan is working. It allows for a methodical process for the social worker to record progress against a set of projected outcomes (or targets). The service user should be encouraged to review both practical and personal outcomes. The starting point of support planning focuses on two key questions:

1. What is important to me?

2. What do I want to change?

Therefore, it remains important that the review considers whether the things that are important to the person have actually been realised and whether this has led to any change(s). This person-centred approach asserts that if we focus on what people want as well as what they need, overall success is more likely (Sanderson, 2000). Obviously, the social worker has a role to play in reviewing how public money has been spent and the impact this has had on the person's well-being and health. The role also involves reviewing the brokerage arrangements and providing support if there are any difficulties or dissatisfaction in this area. It is important that the social worker acknowledges the complexity of arrangements and relationships for individuals using a number of independent agencies and organisations.

Duffy (2010) suggests that the reviewing stage offers the best opportunity to help people make improvements to their lives. He states that once people have had a chance to control their budget, they are in a better position to review what is working and ways things can be improved. At the review stage it is the social worker's role to ensure the service user is remaining in control of their support. To do this, social workers need to adopt an anti-discriminatory approach in their one-to-one work with service users. They also need to demonstrate an awareness of the wider structural issues of power, social exclusion and oppression that impacts upon users dependent on others for their support. This requires the adoption of an anti-oppressive approach, which Braye and Preston-Shoot (2001) describe as one in which they are willing to question and challenge situations in a bid to bring about fundamental changes in power.

RESEARCH SUMMARY

The state of personalisation (Community Care survey) 2013

Community Care undertakes an annual (online) survey of social care professionals' views on personalisation. This sixth survey was answered by 195 social care professionals, all of whom work in English local authorities, 53 per cent defined themselves as social workers (Community Care, 2013). Key consistent themes emerged:

(Continued)

(Continued)

- **Austerity cuts and lack of resources** *84 per cent of practitioners stated that cuts made in the past two years had reduced real choice and control for service users, while 56 per cent felt that the RAS did not effectively allocated money to people in line with their needs. Despite these issues, half of practitioners thought personal budgets would benefit service users in the medium and long term, compared with 22 per cent who thought they would not. Most stated that personal budgets gave users more choice and control than traditionally commissioned care packages – when delivered as a direct payment.*

- **Training and support gaps** *More than half of respondents (56 per cent) stated that they had not had enough training on delivering personal budgets in the past year, while 16 per cent reported not having received any training over that year. Views regarding the quality of training delivered were mixed, 28 per cent saying it was good or very good, 33 per cent poor or very poor and 39 per cent adequate. There was a similar mixture of views on the quality of support from managers on delivering personalisation: 42 per cent stated that they required substantially more training in helping service users build personal and community networks, while a further 35 per cent needed a little more training in this area.*

- **Bureaucracy** *Three out of five respondents (59 per cent) stated that they did not have enough time to effectively support service users through the assessment process. Only 12 per cent said that social workers were trusted to sign off personal budgets up to a certain value without having to refer them to managers or panels. Just 9 per cent of practitioners stated that their RAS was easy for users and carers to understand, and only 22 per cent said it was easy for professionals to understand. Respondents highlighted the levels of bureaucracy involved in assessments and RAS as among the chief barriers to delivering personal budgets effectively – but also claimed that councils were failing to tackle sources of bureaucracy. The need to fill in lengthy forms, use separate forms for assessment, resource allocation and support planning, having to revise inadequate indicative budgets generated by the RAS, cumbersome panel processes for signing off personal budgets, were all cited as sources of unnecessary duplication and 'red tape'.*

- **Limited user involvement** *Almost three-quarters of respondents (72 per cent) said that support planning in their area was usually led by social workers; just 2 per cent said that it was usually led by service users or families; 1 per cent said user-led organisations took the lead. This is despite 15 per cent stating that service users and families were best placed to lead on support planning, 34 per cent saying that it should be left to whomever the service user wanted to take the lead.*

COMMENT

These survey findings are disappointing considering the attention personalisation has been afforded in government policy and the central place it will play in new legislation when the Care Bill becomes law. The implementation of personal budgets is set to carry a legal duty for practitioners charged with assessment of adults with social care needs, yet

72 per cent of survey respondents working in this field felt that the amount of training received was not enough, insufficient or non-existent. The gaps in support and training were accompanied by shortfalls in the skills practitioners felt they needed to deliver on personalisation. These findings appear to indicate that social workers require more community development skills which is seen by the government as important to help develop resilience and independence among older and disabled people, reducing their need for care. In a care and support White Paper (DH, 2012), it promised to work with the College of Social Work to ensure that community development is built into future practice.

Local authorities still need to prioritise training in personalisation despite reduced budgets and necessary cuts. Unlike other areas of social work practice, personalisation is notably different from the approach that many of the current social workers trained under (e.g. care management), so therefore requires dedicated time to explore both ideological and practical implications of practice. Those authorities who have made progress with personalisation have invested in robust training focusing on values, operational issues and building community knowledge, developing person-centred practice and supporting individuals to take control of their own lives when feasible.

Perhaps there are more encouraging signs that the next generation of social workers will be better equipped to adopt more personalised approaches to social work. The College of Social Work (TCSW) and Higher Education Academy (HEA) published a curriculum guide on personalisation (TCSW, 2012) with an expectation that higher education institutions embed this teaching as part of the delivery of the new social work degree. This guide encourages teaching to be designed in a way that enables students to engage critically with the value base, alongside operational issues involved in delivering personalisation (covered in this chapter). So the challenge remains for academics and practice educators to embed this in both undergraduate and post-qualifying teaching and learning.

Personalisation under austerity

The extension of personalisation during a prolonged time of significant cuts in public sector expenditure, resulting in major reductions in local authority budgets, alongside radical social security reforms that significantly impact on people with disabilities, has given rise to much debate. So current austerity measures, following the 2010 Coalition Spending Review, now locates personalisation within a new context where the costs of care and eligibility of those who are entitled to state funding care remain central. While resources always remain limited, personalisation reflects an *aspirational agenda* that has its origins in a more relaxed financial climate than currently prevails (Brookes et al., 2013).

Since 2006 there has been a 22 per cent increase in local authorities who fund only those whose needs are substantial and critical, marking a significant contraction of the population who are eligible for support, and a direct response to the cuts which local authorities are making at the moment (National Audit Office, 2011). Evidence has emerged that the funding being allocated to each individual is decreasing, at a time when the cost of living is rising (Slay, 2011). Vickers et al. (2012) also highlight that there has been little consideration of the needs and experiences of people from black and ethnic minority groups in discussions and research regarding personalisation. There is also evidence of lower engagement with direct payments and personal budgets and the lack of information and knowledge about systems and processes (Needham and Carr, 2009). Ideological criticisms prevail that personalisation continues to represent a move towards privatisation threatening the future of collective social care provision, resulting in greater fragmentation and isolation (Ferguson, 2007).

Previous advocates of personalisation (e.g. Duffy, 2012) caution against a focus on targets rather than entitlements. As local authorities are forced to make efficiency savings (as a consequence of cuts to central government grants), the focus on higher level needs in adult social care means that some users and carers will risk having personal budgets cut and choices restricted as local authorities rationalise commissioning arrangements. Duffy (2012) locates the failure to place entitlements at the heart of personalisation, resulting in a range of operational problems:

- The rationing process (the RAS) is often too bureaucratic and too complex and ambiguous.

- The RAS is also being used to make cuts in ways that seem unreasonable and possibly open to legal challenge.

- The planning process has become more burdensome, with disabled people and families forced to get their own plans through a panel of managers.

- Expensive monitoring systems take away real flexibility and damage independence.

- Little effort has been made to redesign systems to make them more workable for people or social workers.

- Some people are assigned budgets, but lack the means to control them.

CHAPTER SUMMARY

The policy focus on personalisation has undoubtedly resulted in more individuals being able to access better tailored and more innovative provision with service users holding a personal budget reporting higher levels of satisfaction than those relying on traditional services. The impact of resource reductions may not yet be fully felt, but recent research reveals that budget cuts are seen as a potential impediment to future developments. Brookes et al. (2013), for example, identify some innovative practices and approaches to tackling some of the challenges of personalising social care and a real commitment, plus creative lateral thinking, from practitioners and commissioners to find ways of delivering the original underlying ideology and values of this policy.

Bamber, M, Brooks, J, Cusack, S, Edwards, J, Gardner, M, Gridley, K, Howard, L, Marshall, N, Salmon, L and Wood, J (2012) Personalisation in practice, in M Davies (ed.), *Social work with adults*. Basingstoke: Palgrave Macmillan.

A well-crafted, comprehensive up-to-date chapter that covers key themes of personalisation ranging from important theoretical conceptual foundations, legal and policy frameworks, research findings and adult social work practice.

Burton, J, Toscano, T and Zonouzi, M (2012) *Personalisation for social workers: Opportunities and challenges for frontline practice.* Berkshire: Open University Press/McGraw-Hill Education.

An informative text which helpfully contextualises personalisation discussion on real life case studies, ethics, values and service users and carers perspectives plus safeguarding themes. It provides a balanced account of the opportunities and challenges faced by practitioners, commissioners, users, carers, students and researchers engaged in this agenda.

Needham, C (2011) *Personalising public services: Understanding the personalisation narrative.* Bristol: Policy Press.

An up-to-date, topical text written by an accomplished researcher author. Essential reading for any social policy, social work student or academic interested in the critical analysis of personalisation policy in practice.

www.centreforwelfarereform.org

The Centre for Welfare Reform aims to redesign the welfare state in order to increase social justice, promote citizenship, strengthen families and enrich communities. Established by Simon Duffy, it is made up of over 70 international Fellows and has published over 300 publications.

www.in-control.org.uk

In Control is a national charity that aims to create a fairer society where everyone needing additional support has the right, responsibility and freedom to control that support. It provides a range of publications, reports, discussion papers plus useful toolkits to users, carers and practitioners.

www.scie.org.uk

Social Care Institute for Excellence provides excellent online interactive e-learning resources such as the What is personalisation, Putting personalisation into practice and Fair access to care services training modules. SCIE also provides a diversity of accessible practice briefings and guides as well as Social Care TV which explores personalisation from particular user and carer perspectives.

Chapter 4

Service user groups and personalisation

Ali Gardner

Introduction

This chapter explores the experience of personalisation and self-directed support from the perspective of the different service user groups. Personal budgets continue to increase in councils across England. Figures from the NHS Information Centre show that the numbers receiving personal budgets increased from 377,000 to 527,000 between 2010/11 and 2011/12 (NHS Information Centre, 2013). This represents a massive increase since 2003, when a total of 60 people in six pilot projects were receiving personal budgets (Tyson et al., 2010). Throughout this chapter I will be referring to several evaluations that have been carried out since 2003, including reports from In Control, at three stages of their pilot projects (Poll et al., 2006; Hatton et al., 2008; Tyson et al., 2010), the national evaluation of individual budgets carried out by the Department of Health, frequently referred to as the IBSEN study (Glendinning et al., 2008), and the 2013 TLAP National Personal Budgets Survey. These evaluations are sources of valuable information relating to service users' experiences of personal budgets and self-directed support, although it is argued that there are different terms of reference among these different evaluations. While the In Control evaluations aim to evaluate the experiences of self-directed support, the IBSEN study also endeavours to evaluate the integration of different funding streams with social care budgets, leading to a more complex picture (Glasby and Littlechild, 2009). The TLAP survey aims to capture people's lived experience of self-directed support and provide councils with a way of measuring and understanding their performance. The data, therefore, from all of these evaluations requires careful and considered scrutiny. As with any evaluative research, it is important to be aware of the underpinning ideology informing the research. Also, to recognise the potential for bias within self-selected pilots – local authorities may volunteer to participate in a pilot project for a variety of pragmatic and economic reasons, in addition to aspirations to improve their service provision. Additionally, service users may come forward because they are particularly disenchanted with current provision, and therefore they may have an intrinsic motivation to make self-directed support work (Glasby and Littlechild, 2009).

At this stage it is useful to consider the background to these evaluations in some more detail before examining the findings in relation to the specific service user groups.

The IBSEN study

Before focusing on the most recent findings from the TLAP national survey, it is worth reflecting on the key findings from the IBSEN study in 2005 and the work of In Control and their pilot projects. Individual budgets were piloted in 13 local authorities across England between 2005 and 2007. In addition to introducing new arrangements for assessment, resource allocation and support planning, the pilots were tasked with bringing together several different funding streams and integrating their respective assessment processes. The pilots were subject to a comprehensive evaluation by IBSEN (individual budgets evaluation network) team.

IBSEN aimed to identify whether individual budgets (IBs) offer a better way of supporting disabled adults and older people than conventional methods of resource allocation and service delivery. IBSEN evaluation was a randomised controlled trial. This large-scale study of the costs, outcomes and cost effectiveness of IBs was complemented by process evaluations of the implementation of IBs, conducted through interviews with key local authority managers and front-line staff; and by in-depth interviews with a sub-sample of people recently offered IBs.

It was found that IBs were generally welcomed by service users because they offered more opportunity for choice and control over support arrangements than conventional social care arrangements. However, there were variations in outcomes between different groups of IB users; satisfaction was highest among mental health service users and physically disabled adults of working age and lowest among older people. The costs of IBs were lowest for mental health service users and highest for people with learning disabilities. IBs appeared to be cost-effective in relation to social outcomes, but not for psychological well-being. For older people, there was no difference in social care outcomes between IBs and conventional services. In order to find out more about perceived strengths and weaknesses of IBs and the differences between service user groups, it will be useful to consult the full report (available at **www.york.ac.uk/spru**).

The IBSEN study remains an influential piece of evaluation and it has provided a wealth of knowledge and led to the development of policy, practice guidance and further research relating to this new approach: for example, shaping the Department of Health approach to piloting and evaluation of NHS personal health budgets; evidence from the evaluation on the integration of funding streams shaped the Department for Work and Pension's *Right to control* trailblazer pilot projects that were introduced by the Welfare Reform Act 2009; the Audit Commission drew on the IBSEN evaluation to shape its investigation into the financial management of personal budgets (Audit Commission, 2010); the development of a *personalisation toolkit* for local authorities was informed by the learning from the evaluation.

In Control

In Control is a national programme which aims to change the organisation of social care in England so that people who use support can take more control of their lives (NIMHE, 2006). While the evaluation of In Control's first phase, 2003–05, was based on a small sample of 31 people with learning disabilities to assess the impact of self-directed support on their lives, the findings indicated that self-directed support had the potential to promote choice and control, and satisfaction with support received (Poll et al., 2006). The evaluation of the second phase, 2005–07, involved a larger sample of 196 service users with personal budgets across 17 local authorities in England. Within this sample group, 58 per cent had learning difficulties, 20 per cent had physical disabilities, and older people represented the remaining 13 per cent of the sample (Hatton et al., 2008). Again there were encouraging findings, with participants reporting either positive changes or no changes in relation to the domains of health and well-being, relationships, quality of life, choice and control, participation in community life, feeling of security at home, personal dignity in support, and economic well-being (Carr and Robbins, 2009). However, the authors of this evaluation stressed that the study had limitations as the sample was not necessarily representative, and people with learning disabilities or physical disabilities were more likely to report improvements than the small numbers of older people who participated (Glasby and Littlechild, 2009).

In Control has published an evaluation of the third phase, from 2008 to 2009. Over two-thirds of the local authorities participating in this evaluation provided a breakdown of personal budget recipients by service user group, indicating that 23 per cent had physical disabilities, 18 per cent had learning disabilities, 6 per cent had mental health problems, and older people represented the remaining 53 per cent. The aggregated findings from this phase and phase two are presented (Tyson et al., 2010). The resulting data is not subdivided into service user groups. Rather, the results are presented as data relating to the overall uptake of personal budgets from a participant group of between 385 and 522 people, and the impact of these personal budgets on their lives. The findings are positive, with 66 per cent of the participant group reporting that the control they had over their support had improved, and 68 per cent reporting that their overall quality of life had improved since receiving personal budgets; 58 per cent reported spending more time with people they wanted to, and also taking a more active role in their community; 55 per cent felt that they were supported with more dignity, and 51 per cent reported feeling in better health.

The TLAP National Personal Budgets Survey

TLAP funded Lancaster University and In Control to undertake a survey with 22 volunteer councils in England in 2012–13. In total 2,022 personal budget holders completed the survey (with 20 councils having more than 50 respondents). In addition 1,386 carers completed the survey (with 15 councils having more than 50 respondents).

The personal budgets outcomes and evaluation tool (POET) aims to gather views and experiences from personal budget holders, their families and carers. It is designed to measure how well the council is managing to implement personal budgets and to what effect. The tool asks service users and carers about the impact of personal budgets in important areas of their lives and support. It also gives them a chance to express their views about outcomes and process.

In this section, a summary of the findings from the survey is presented, but it will also be useful for you to consult the full report (which can be found at **www. thinklocalactpersonal.org.uk**).

The following 14 outcomes were measured as part of the POET survey:

1. Physical health

2. Mental well-being

3. Being in control of life

4. Being independent

5. Being in control of support

6. Getting the support you need

7. Being supported with dignity

8. Feeling safe

9. Choose where you live/who you live with

10. Get/keep paid job (not measured for older people)

11. Volunteering and helping community

12. Relations with family

13. Relations with friends

14. Relations with paid supporters

The measurement of these outcomes enabled further exploration in relation to six key questions, which will now be addressed.

1. **What is the balance of good versus poor experiences of personal budgets?**

Overall, less that 10 per cent of personal budget holders reported a negative impact on any of the 14 areas that they were asked about (see Table 4.1).

Table 4.1 Reported impacts

Reported impact by personal budget holders	Percentage
Reported *positive* impact on:	70%
• being as independent as you want to be • getting the support you need and want • being supported with dignity	
Reported *positive* impact on:	60%
• physical health • mental well-being • control over important things in life • control over your support	
Reported *positive* impact on:	50%
• feeling safe in and outside your home • relationships with paid supporters	
Reported *no difference* in:	50%
• choosing where to live/who to live with • relationships with family • relationships with friends	
Reported *no difference* in:	80%
• getting and keeping a paid job • volunteering	

2. **Do personal budgets work better for some groups of people than others?**

The survey numbers allowed comparisons between: older people, working age adults with learning disabilities, working age adults with mental health issues and working age disabled adults. Analysis showed that in the following eight areas there seemed to be an equal impact across the groups:

• Physical health.

• Being as independent as you want to be.

• Getting the support you need and want.

• Being supported with dignity.

• Feeling safe in and outside your home.

- Choosing where to live/who to live with.

- Getting and keeping a paid job.

- Relationships with family.

In some areas there were some differences. Personal budgets were less likely to make a difference for older people in the following areas:

- Mental well-being.

- Control over your support.

- Volunteering.

- Relationships with friends.

- Relationships with paid supporters.

3. **Is it important to know how much is in your budget and do more expensive personal budgets work better?**

Over 70 per cent of personal budget holders in the survey knew the amount of their budget with no difference across social care groups. People with council-managed budgets were less likely to know the amount compared to people with other types of budget.

Of those who could estimate their budget amounts, Table 4.2 highlights the value of budgets per service user group.

Table 4.2 Value of budgets per service user group

Service user group	Estimated value of weekly budget (average)
Physical disabilities	£200
Learning disabilities	£170
Older people	£121
Mental health issues	£90

The survey also revealed differences in value of budget depending on the type of budget (see Table 4.3).

Table 4.3 Value of budget depending on type

Type of budget	Estimated value of weekly budget (average)
Direct payments looked after by someone else	£171
Individual service funds	£146
Direct payments to the person	£138
Managed personal budgets	£120

- Knowing the amount of personal budgets was associated strongly with better outcomes for people with learning disabilities and physical disabilities though much less so for older people and people with mental health issues.

- Analysis showed no linear relationship between costs and outcomes for any type of personal budget for any of the outcomes.

4. **Do particular types of personal budgets work better than others?**

The type of budget was found to have varying impacts on different areas of life. Council-managed personal budgets were *less likely* than other types to have a positive impact (i.e. more likely to make no difference) on:

- Mental well-being.

- Control over important things in life.

- Being as independent as you want to be.

- Control over your support.

- Getting the support you need and want.

- Being supported with dignity.

- Feeling safe in and outside your home.

- Relationships with family, friends and paid supporters.

5. **Do personal budgets using self-directed support processes work better?**

This question revealed an important finding. For most aspects of the personal budget process and most outcomes, there were big differences across the councils. The analysis showed that councils find some aspects of the process more difficult than others. However, the best councils performed well even in the more difficult aspects of the process. For all social care groups, the idea of councils making the personal budget process easier was robustly associated with better outcomes for personal budget holders.

A total of 488 personal budget holders made written comments. Responses tended to report more extreme experiences, either positive or negative, meaning that the findings were mixed, but it is possible to identify that 60 per cent of the responses relating to the *process* were broadly negative and 97 per cent of responses relating to impact on life were positive. People's comments covered a wide range of concerns, but the majority could be categorised into the three main themes (see Table 4.4).

Impact on carers

The survey was completed by 1,386 carers. Most carers of personal budget holders also reported positive experiences (though to a lesser extent than the personal budget user themselves). Table 4.5 outlines some of the key findings.

Table 4.4 Three main themes

Theme	Comments
Personal circumstances	• Nature/extent of disability and how it affected life • Importance of family relationships
Personal budget process	• Experience of taking control of budget, including assessment, support planning, acquiring and directing support • Experience of staff encountered • Complexity and timeliness of process • Availability of information and advice
Impact on life	• On themselves and those around them • Importance of having personalised care and support • Concerns and hopes for future • Importance of independent living • Making key decisions • Being in their own home • Taking part in community

Table 4.5 Key findings

Key finding	%
Reported that views were included in their personal budget holder's support plan	**77%**
Reported that the personal budget made their (the carer's) life better in four of the nine areas asked about:	
1. Finances	**52%**
2. Having the support you need to continue caring and remain well	**69%**
3. Carer's quality of life	**60%**
4. Carer's physical and mental well-being	**53%**

Comments written by carers reinforced and extended these conclusions. Carers were often highly positive about the impact of personal budgets on the lives of the personal budget holder, themselves as carers and other family members. However, they were all negative about all aspects of the personal budget process and the stress they associated with this process. Carers of older people were least likely to report improvements as a result of a personal budget.

Finally, the survey was completed by 195 personal health budget holders and 117 carers across 12 sites. The key findings from this part of the evaluation can be found below in the section on 'Health'.

Impact on future policy and practice

The findings from the survey are likely to play an important role in shaping future policy and practice in social care. In particular, TLAP along with other key stakeholders will be looking towards ways in which the findings can shape regulations and guidance for the Care Bill and subsequent legislation. Likewise, a key role for TLAP is to work in partnership to support the delivery of personalisation. It is important again to remind ourselves that personal budgets are only one aspect of personalisation, and a focus, therefore, on broader elements including co-production, market and provider development, information and advice are centrally important in achieving the principles of personalisation. Furthermore, there is a clear danger of striving only to achieve target numbers of personal budgets, as this does not guarantee a real transfer of power to people using social care or the extension of choice and control. As can be seen from the findings of this survey, those on council-managed budgets were less likely to know the value of their budget and were less likely to experience a positive impact in key areas of their life as a result of receiving one. These findings have to be seriously challenged if personal budgets can be measured as a key *marker* in achieving personalisation. Given that the recent ADASS survey, *A bleak outlook is getting bleaker* (2013), reported that one of the three areas likely to be *highly important* as aids to saving resources in the coming year was *increased personalisation* (identified by 47 per cent of directors), it is crucial that the government and policy-makers carefully consider the medium and long-term outlook and possibilities in relation to personal budgets and avoid the temptation of seeing it as an instant panacea.

Emerging areas of personalisation

It is perhaps no surprise that personalisation and self-directed support has taken off in areas such as disability and mental health where there is a strong history of service user voice and social movement activity promoting notions of independence, choice and control. It is interesting to note that the successes and principles of personalisation are now being adopted in other public service areas, some of which will require significant individual, organisational, cultural, societal and paradigm shifts if they are to be taken seriously and embedded within practice. For some organisations, such as the NHS, the concept of directing, purchasing and managing one's own support/treatment is clearly more challenging than arranging someone to provide support to prepare a meal. For other organisations, for example those connected to the criminal justice system, the concept of *allowing* people to choose and direct their own rehabilitation and recovery using *tax payers' money* in the form of a personal budget potentially presents very different challenging questions. While social care was not immune to practice dilemmas concerning questions of care versus control, deserving versus undeserving and the notion of professional expertise, they are perhaps amplified when we begin to think about medical treatment or providing money to someone who has broken the law. In this next section we explore some of the areas in which personalisation is beginning to emerge and consider the key opportunities and obstacles in assessing whether it can be a reality. It is not possible to cover all areas of emerging practice and development in relation to personalisation and self-directed support; instead I will focus on four areas where the research and policy development is making personalisation a reality in practice: health, housing, homelessness, criminal justice, and disabled children and their families.

Health

The government has committed the NHS to rolling out personal health budgets across England. By April 2014 all clinical commissioning groups will need to be able to offer personal health budgets to people receiving NHS Continuing Healthcare, and by 2015 everyone who could benefit will have the option of a personal health budget (TLAP, 2013a).

This policy direction has largely been driven by the findings of the POET survey (TLAP, 2013b), which as well as social care focused on the experience of 195 individuals holding a personal health budget. Some of the major findings from this strand of the study include:

- Personal health budget holders reported a wide range of primary long-term conditions for which they held their budget (27.3 per cent), a mental health condition (12.3 per cent), learning disabilities (7.8 per cent), stroke (5.6 per cent) or tetraplegic conditions (5.6 per cent).

- People most commonly managed their personal health budgets through direct payments paid to them (30.8 per cent), followed by direct payments looked after by a broker (29.7 per cent), council or NHS-managed personal health budgets (13.3 per cent), service provider-managed personal health budgets (12.3 per cent), direct payments looked after by a family member or friend (11.3 per cent); 5.6 per cent of people did not know how their personal health budget was managed.

- 80 per cent of personal health budget holders reported having been told their weekly support costs. For the 117 people who could provide an estimate of the annual cost of their personal health budget, the median estimated value was £2,340 per year. People holding some form of direct payment tended to have more expensive budgets that people with managed budgets

In terms of the impact of a personal health budget, over 70 per cent of personal health budget holders reported it having a positive impact on their independence and over 60 per cent reported their budget having a positive impact on their physical health, being supported with dignity and respect, being in control of their support, their mental health and well-being and other important things in life. Over 80 per cent felt confident that their needs would be met by a personal health budget, and factors robustly associated with positive outcomes for personal health budget holders included holding the personal health budget in the form of a direct payment paid to family/friends; knowing the amount; having help to plan from family and friends; feeling their views were included in their support plan; and organisations making aspects of the personal health budget process easier. Similarly, carers of people holding personal health budgets generally reported personal health budgets as having a positive impact on their quality of life (70.2 per cent), support for them to continue caring (67.6 per cent) and their finances (60.2 per cent).

Attempts to integrate health, care and support are a regular feature in government policy and legislation relating to this area, yet repeatedly the experience of service users is that the lack of integration creates serious difficulties (Beresford and Hasler, 2009). Service users cited the lack of communication between agencies, flexibility and taking responsibility between agencies meaning that care and support was often fragmented, delayed or duplicated, leading to the escalation of support required (Beresford and Andrews, 2012). Ever mindful of the changing demography of the country, in particular the healthier lives people are leading than ever before, due largely to progressive knowledge and technologies, the current government is acutely aware of the challenges this progress brings. People are living longer, with more complex needs that require constant care and attention, and disabled children with complex needs are living longer and more positive lives. The recent publication *Integrated care and support: Our shared commitment* (DH, 2013) provides a framework document on integration. Key national partners have signed up to finding ways of using existing structures such as *health and well-being boards* to bring together local authorities, the NHS, care and support providers, education, housing services and public health to make further steps towards integration. Key messages in this document include the need to develop person-centred, co-ordinated services, engaging with and listening to local people, patients and people who use services, and developing the joint allocation of resources. It remains to be seen whether the language of personalisation which is so readily used within government policy can translate into practice, as suggested by Care and Support Minister Norman Lamb, to *make joined-up and co-ordinated health and care the norm by 2018* (*Guardian*, 2013).

In response to the government's commitment to roll out personal health budgets and the national evaluation of the personal health budgets, Mind (2013) reported on their own research with people with mental health problems to find out what they wanted from services and support and what role personal health budgets might play. In particular, Mind wanted to consider the role that personal health budgets could play in light of high levels of dissatisfaction among people from some black and minority ethnic (BME) groups with mental health services and their disproportionate experiences of inpatient care, detention and compulsion.

The report is based on research undertaken by Mind from June to October 2012, including an online survey completed by 502 people, two focus groups, interviews with people currently using personal health budgets, and interviews with national and local stakeholders. Findings from the research highlighted lack of information, long waits for psychological treatments, lack of choice, lack of involvement and lack of attention to cultural needs. The research unsurprisingly found that choice and control are of particularly high importance in mental health where high levels of compulsion are common and the power imbalance between patients and professionals is particularly pronounced. For example, 77 per cent of respondents to the survey said that being able to choose the type of treatment/services they could access was very important to them, as was the choice of professional (61 per cent). However, respondents suggested that choice of treatment was uncommon (11 per cent) and only 6 per cent responded that they had a choice of the professional who treated them.

People from the BME communities spoke of the importance of all services being culturally sensitive. For some people this included the choice of being supported by someone from the same culture or community, while others preferred to use mainstream services but wanted a greater understanding of their cultural and spiritual needs within those services.

Some of the barriers to making personal health budgets work in mental health were identified within the research. Respondents to the survey reported that they might struggle to access a budget without ongoing support. People from BME communities may face additional barriers in accessing services and support either due to lack of knowledge about existing services or because existing services are not linguistically or culturally appropriate for them. In their recommendations, Mind suggested that personal health budgets could be a powerful tool in addressing some of the existing ethnic inequalities in mental healthcare, enabling people from BME communities to access services and support before they reach crisis point and empowering them to purchase support that meets their cultural needs. Attention to good support planning and brokerage for BME communities was similarly identified as being crucial in making personal health budgets a reality for this group of people.

The research suggests that there is limited awareness and understanding of personal health budgets among potential budget holders. Only 12 per cent of respondents to the survey said that they had a good understanding of personal health budgets, while 47 per cent had never heard of them before. Respondents expressed many concerns and misconceptions about what budgets would be and how they would be affected by them, including eligibility queries, unfair assessments that dismiss or minimise mental health, the burden of managing a budget and fear it would be too stressful, the high levels of bureaucracy, a worry of exceeding the budget and having to pay the shortfall, and a worry that this was the first step towards privatisation, leading to a gradual reduction in universal services.

The research informed the following recommendations from Mind in supporting personal budgets to work in mental health:

- The implementation of holistic needs assessments to determine eligibility for personal health budgets, including hidden symptoms and fluctuating conditions which mirrors the right that NHS Continuing Healthcare patients will have from April 2014.

- The development of best practice guidance that specifically addresses the specific issues for those who are most marginalised, including people with mental health problems and people from BME communities. The location of this material must be carefully planned to enhance the likelihood of people from these groups finding out about personal health budgets.

- Further development of brokerage, support planning and peer support specific to people with mental health problems and attention to specific cultural or linguistic needs of people from BME communities.

- Identifying and sharing the specific ways people with mental health problems spend their personal health budgets to inform future commissioning.

- Widen the evidence base to include more research into social and non-traditional interventions for mental health, including qualitative research focused on patient outcomes and experiences.

- Assess and plan for the wider roll-out of personal health budgets from 2014 and the implications of potential double-running costs and ensuring the continued existence of traditional services that some people may always choose.

- Explore how budgets in health and social care can be integrated at a local level, in recognition that the divide between the two is not very meaningful to people with mental health problems and to avoid duplication of assessment.

Housing

The call for personalisation has grown over two decades and has survived changes in government. As it evolves, so does interest from a range of other public sectors. Over the last five years, interest in the potential of personalisation within the housing and homelessness sector has emerged. In 2013, Stephens and Michaelson reported on the findings of the three-year Up2Us project, supported by the New Economics Foundation (NEF), involving six pilot schemes across the country investigating personalisation in housing care and support. Each pilot tested ways of bringing people together to pool money in order to buy the care and support that they want.

Some of the practical activity involved:

- The development of a community networking portal bringing together local people, local knowledge and local resources.
- Residents sharing activities in Extra Care housing and playing a role in commissioning future services.
- Young people with a history of homelessness making purchases to improve their health and well-being.
- Setting up user-run co-operatives with members taking part in activities in the evenings and at weekends.
- Jointly buying gym equipment.
- Jointly commissioning overnight support.
- Using participatory budgeting to organise day centre activities.

At the heart of all these activities, housing associations charged with facilitating the projects were set a clear expectation that all activities should be based on the principles of co-production and that the people who use the services should be at the centre of each pilot scheme. NEF worked alongside the pilot sites as a critical friend, tracking development, drawing out lessons, feeding them back to participants and building knowledge about what works and what doesn't. A well-being questionnaire was completed by Up2Us participants and further well-being analysis was conducted on the qualitative findings.

The following key messages were reported in the final report *Buying things together: A review of the Up2Us approach*.

1. Decouple personalisation and personal budgets. Developing a personalised way of working that puts the individual in control is possible and desirable, regardless of the individual's funding package.
2. Take an asset-based approach. Understand what people are good at, and benefiting from their skills and lived experiences makes interventions more effective for everyone.
3. Develop personalised practice in organisation procedures, inspection and auditing regimes. Organisations involved must support cultural and systemic changes needed for personalisation to flourish.

4. Support initiatives from bottom up whereby those who use services choose and direct how money is spent.

5. Prioritise approaches that maintain and grow people's well-being, including activities that foster strong social relationships between people and give people a sense of autonomy, control, safety and security.

The overwhelming message from the report was that choice is extremely important. While the pilot demonstrated that there was great potential for collective purchasing, it recognised that this must be identified and directed by the people who use the services rather than others trying to impose expertise.

Homelessness

In 2008, the previous government published their *Rough sleeping strategy* (DCLG, 2008). As part of this strategy, with the aim of putting an end to rough sleeping by 2012, a 15-point action plan was agreed. Action point 9 read:

> We will provide more personalised services including testing individual budgets to increase the control people have over the services they need.

Following on from this commitment, the DCLG commissioned four *rough sleeping personalisation projects* across England to explore the effectiveness of personalisation for homeless people. The pilots focused initially on small numbers of people who had slept rough for many years and up until this point been unwilling to accept help. The model used tried to incorporate flexibility and choice as an individual budget to try to find new solutions.

Personalised support for rough sleepers
J Hough and B Rice (2010) *Providing personalised support to rough sleepers: An evaluation of the City of London pilot.*

This piece of action research, conducted by Joseph Rowntree Foundation, evaluated the impact of a pilot project offering personal budgets to rough sleepers in the City of London and explored reasons for the success of the project delivered by Broadway, a London-based homelessness charity, 13 months after the start of the project.

- 15 people who had been sleeping rough for between four and 45 years were offered a personal budget with a maximum of £3,000 per person. Typically people spent the money on furniture and comforts such as a TV, to pay off small arrears, buy gas or electricity, buy food, pay to join courses.

- A full time co-ordinator offered support to the person in identifying a broker or supporting the individual to design a support plan.

- The co-ordinator also offered one-to-one support to participants during and after resettlement.

- By the time of the evaluation, the majority were in accommodation (7) or making plans to move into accommodation (2).

Findings

- Those who moved off the streets talked positively about their lives in accommodation and included references to making future plans, taking courses, reconnecting with families, and addressing physical, mental and drug and alcohol problems.

- Several participants highlighted the long-term personalised support after resettlements in the form of a dedicated worker as essential to maintaining their tenancies.

- Everyone involved, including the service users and the professionals, believed that personalised approaches could work for rough sleepers.

- The approach brought people elements of choice and control that were not provided by standard offers of support, alongside intensive support from one trusted worker.

Many homeless organisations, providing support to a range of service user groups, have adopted the personalised approach within different settings such as hostels, floating support and shared housing. It will be useful to take time to explore the different ways that organisations have developed personalisation with homeless people. Homeless Link, an organisation representing and supporting 500 organisations working with homeless people in the UK, provides a wealth of information about the projects currently being undertaken and the future direction in relation to personalisation (**www.homelesslink.org.uk**).

While the current government continues to tackle rough sleeping, as suggested in their report *Vision to end rough sleeping* (HM Government, 2011), which makes six commitments to tackle homelessness, there is no specific reference to personalisation or personal budgets within the report.

Criminal justice

The high reoffending rate among prisoners in England and Wales continues to challenge governments, and numerous ideological and policy shifts have largely failed to reduce it. Sixty per cent of offenders leaving prison reoffend within 12 months, a figure that has remained fairly stable since 2000 (Ministry of Justice, 2012). In the same period there has been a growing interest in developing alternative conceptualisations of offending behaviour generally, and in particular, notions of *assisting desistance* are increasingly being incorporated into offender management practices (Dickie, 2013). The central tenets of personalisation align closely with the framework for assisting desistance in terms of individualised approaches which build on strengths, respect and individual agency rather than needs and risks (Weaver and McNeil, 2007; McNeil et al., 2012).

The following example illustrates the practical application of personalisation within the criminal justice system.

ACTIVITY **4.1**

As you read this next couple of paragraphs, make a note of any observations, reactions, opportunities or challenges you sense as you think about the example provided. Think about your own reaction and that of the general public.

Personalisation at HMP Everthorpe

The personalisation project at HMP Everthorpe was established as part of the Revolving Doors Agency's National Development Programme. The project was developed in partnership by HMP Everthorpe, In Control, Hull City Council, and Yorkshire and Humber Improvement Partnership. It was delivered by Goodwin Development Trust.

The service was devised to work with prisoners who were failing to engage with conventional resettlement services and focused on prisoners over the age of 21 serving sentences of less than 12 months, as this was the group with the highest reoffending rates. The model was informed by a piece of action research, *Getting a blue life* (Moore and Nicoll, 2009), which explored with prisoners and staff the potential opportunities and barriers in adopting a personalised approach in prison resettlement. Prisoners participating in this research explored issues they believed promoted or prevented their offending, such as early childhood experiences, family relationships, having a home or a job, etc. The service model that followed involved a dedicated project worker who acted as an advocate, provided support to participants in developing a life plan and building support networks, and finally facilitating access to a beneficiary fund to assist participants in realising their life plans. Although the project faced some unforeseeable challenges, such as a change in personnel and ultimate disbandment of the organisation leading the project, along with teething problems relating to sourcing suitable support material, the project eventually worked intensively with 29 participants between April 2011 and April 2012 who were seeking to address a range of issues including housing, substance misuse, mental health, finances and debt, and employment, training and education.

Using the Outcomes Star assessment tool that is widely used in working with vulnerable groups, participants positioned themselves on a ten-point ladder of change from dependence to independence across the following key areas: motivation and taking responsibility; self-care and living skills; managing money and personal administration; social networking and relationships; drug and alcohol misuse; physical health; emotional and mental health; meaningful use of time; managing tenancy and accommodation; and offending.

The participant-led assessment was administered at the point of their first engagement with the project and repeated at subsequent intervals to capture movement along the Outcomes Star ladder during the period participants were in custody and after release.

Findings

The greatest increases were recorded in the areas of motivation and taking responsibility, emotional and mental health, and meaningful use of time. The notion of motivation and taking responsibility is closely aligned to the principle of personalisation, in so much as placing choice and control in the hands of service users. Participants reported on the importance of this aspect and associated it with having the opportunity to actively create change for oneself rather than going along with help. The greatest increase across all ten areas of the Outcomes Star was recorded in participants' perceptions of their emotional well-being and mental health and how well they felt able to manage these. They commented positively about the opportunity of having someone to talk to and a source of support at difficult times.

A central function of the project worker's role was to support participants in identifying their strengths and to assist them in developing plans to build on their interests after release. At this point the project worker facilitated the participants in accessing the beneficiary fund. Examples of the use of the beneficiary fund to support participants in achieving their goals included:

- Three months' car insurance for a formerly self-employed plasterer to re-establish himself in the trade, in order to be able to transport his tools around.

- A bike, purchased from the prison bicycle repair scheme, for a participant living on the outskirts of the city to deliver his CV in looking for employment.

- Registering at a local college to finish a computer course that had been started while in prison.

- Rebuilding relationships to spend time with formerly estranged children.

Finally, the findings did point towards the potential for a personalised approach to resettlement to impact on a range of health and well-being outcomes. Improved scores on the Outcomes Star in relation to offending behaviour were recorded among the cohort in the period during custody. However, average scores in relation to the offending measure subsequently dropped in the period following release but remained above the average offending score recorded at first contact with the project. A more robust measure of the impact in reoffending was not possible within the parameters of the project, given the small size of the sample and the limited timeframe.

COMMENT

Some of the more general lessons from this project mirror many of the challenges faced by the social care sector. First, overcoming the cultural shift required to implement personalisation was a steep learning curve for the project delivery team. Breaking from established working practices in a very controlled setting to adopt an approach based on sharing power and taking unknown risks was a challenging task in the timeframe available. Similarly, the responsibility to facilitate the beneficiary fund was difficult for the delivery team as they needed to decide what was acceptable to agree and what should be declined. Clearly, decisions surrounding the allocation of public money are contentious and this has been a constant feature in social care. Such dilemmas for delivery staff and those with financial responsibilities in the public sector can only be amplified for those in the criminal justice system where principles of rehabilitation, recovery and punishment in relation to the purpose of prisons continue to be highly contested by the public.

ACTIVITY **4.2**

Having learned about the work undertaken in this project, read the following quote and first write down your personal response to this. Be as honest as you can be. Now think about your professional response as a social worker. Is it different or the same?

> Imprisonment is designed to take away choice, at least those choices which might endanger the public. It is therefore necessarily de-humanising. But it may also take away other choices, so that prisons can run safely. There should be no need to take away yet further choices … if you can give more responsibility, the more responsible behaviour is likely to result. And if you deny responsibility to people you cannot blame them for behaving irresponsibly.

(Pryor, 2001, pp. 1, 4)

COMMENT

It is important that we are mindful of our own personal responses and develop an awareness of how these may impact on our professional responses. Similarly, it is important to consider how perceptions and attitudes towards criminal justice will differ in society and recognise how challenging it can be for individuals, organisation and policy-makers to develop services and agree eligibility when they have to consider, balance and ultimately decide how public money is spent and the extent to which the rights of those who have broken the law should be granted or denied.

Disabled children and their families

Since the introduction of the Carers and Disabled Children Act 2000, the parents of disabled children have been able to access direct payments to support them in their role. The previous government pledged to trial the individual budget approach and committed to the principle of extending self-directed support for families with disabled children in *Improving the life chances of disabled people* (Prime Minister's Strategy Unit, 2005), and subsequently the *Aiming high for disabled children* strategy (AHDC) (Department for Education, 2007) sought to take forward this recommendation. The current government continues to progress this approach, and in the publication of the Green Paper *Support and aspiration* (Department for Education, 2011) followed by the *Progress and next steps* document (Department for Education, 2012), they set out an ambitious programme of service transformation for children with spe-cial educational needs, their families and disabled children's services. This programme of change consists of many different elements including workforce change, the role of the private and voluntary sector, new approaches to assessment and planning and the introduction of personal budgets across social care, health and education.

A wider concept of personalisation is set to be extended for children with special edu-cational needs, their families and disabled children's services generally. Some of the specific changes, which have been included in the Children and Families Bill (2013) (at the time of writing this is in the House of Lords waiting for its second reading) include:

- From 2014, Statements of Special Educational Needs will be replaced by Education, Health and Care Plans that will come out of a Single Assessment process; these plans will only apply to children with multiple health and learning needs. From birth to the age of 25, children meeting these criteria will have a personal budget that covers education, health and social care needs.

- The introduction of the *local offer* will help to identify the support and services available across education, health and social care within each local author-ity area. It will clearly state the criteria for the services and how they can be accessed. This aim of the local offer is to support disabled children, and their families, who do not meet the local authority eligibility criteria for a personal budget.

Much of the development work around disabled children and personalisation has been led and informed by In Control. In this stream of work, In Control have attempted to conceptualise and promote personalisation as a whole system of change rather than become preoccupied with the money or just the personal budget as has been witnessed in adult social care (Crosby et al., 2012). The move to a joined-up approach across health education and social care, suggests Crosby, requires a new relationship between statutory agencies, services and children and families. The new relationship is based on an approach which sees:

- *The child and the family at the centre* This involves seeing disabled children and their families as the experts.

- *The recognition of a family's real wealth* The child and the family will have a range of existing resources that they can draw upon. They may need support to enable them to utilise these resources.

- *A whole system* All support needs a joined-up approach focused on strategic outcomes.

- *Clear and simple outcomes* These should be agreed at the outset, simply stat-ing what services will achieve for young people and their families.

- *A simple pathway* An easy, clear and accessible process for how children will be assessed, the eligibility criteria, allocation of personal budget and review.

CHAPTER SUMMARY

This chapter has explored the recent national and local evaluations of personal budgets for a range of service user and carer groups. A clear message from this process is that the notion of choice and control are central to the success of self-directed support and that robust, clear, accessible, equitable systems are required in order for people to make informed choices and take control of their own support.

It is interesting to note that a change of government taking place midway through several of these strands of work does not appear to have interrupted the flow or pace of extending personalisation at a policy or practice level.

The emergence of other areas of practice such as health, housing, criminal justice and disabled children is interesting as we grapple with issues of care versus control, deserving versus undeserving and professional expert versus personal expert. The development of personalisation in the social care sector has tackled many of these issues along the way, and this learning can be used positively in tackling some of the more tricky issues we may encounter when considering the higher stakes presented in more contentious areas such as medical treatment or providing financial support to those within the criminal justice system.

Finally, the body of research and literature now building in these relatively new areas provides a solid basis to ensure that research-informed practice is a central platform for future services.

FURTHER READING

Glasby, J and Littlechild, R (2009) *Direct payments and personal budgets: Putting personalisation into practice.* Bristol: Policy Press.

This book is an invaluable resource for everyone interested in personalisation. It summarises the current evidence in relation to direct payments and personal budgets, and considers some of the challenges inherent in the implementation of self-directed support.

Leece, J and Bornat, J (eds) (2006) *Developments in direct payments.* Bristol: Policy Press.

This book provides you with the opportunity to consider and compare the experiences of providers and service users in relation to direct payments. It also compares developments in the UK with those in North America.

WEBSITES

www.in-control.org.uk

This website contains a wealth of information relating to policy, practice and experience from people directing their own support.

www.thinklocalactpersonal.org.uk

TLAP Access to the national personal budgets survey 2013.

www.york.ac.uk/spru

The Social Policy Research Unit has an international reputation for excellence in research. This website contains many of the key studies and also useful articles relating to personalisation.

www.ncil.org/

The National Centre for Independent Living website contains valuable information relating to independent living, direct payments and personal budgets.

www.mind.org.uk/

There is a wealth of information on this website relating to personalisation including access to the 2013 research project relating to personal budgets.

Chapter 5
Service user narrative

Ali Gardner

Introduction

This chapter provides an opportunity to hear directly from individuals directing their own support. It would be impossible to write a book about personalisation without contributions from individuals. Listening to their experiences provides us with an opportunity to gain some insight into how this agenda is changing the lives of individuals in need of social care.

Social work textbooks regularly provide case studies to aid student learning. Typically students are given a set of circumstances followed by a number of questions in relation to the social work role. In seminars, it is common for students to be asked to break into small groups and work through information, suggesting how the social worker should intervene to support the individual in need. We must, however, acknowledge that the relationship being crafted here between social worker and service user is based on an underlying assumption that the social worker knows best. In this process of learning, students are being trained to respond to information rather than individuals. This probably seems a little strange as many of the scenarios will include a focus on anti-discriminatory practice and empowerment. This juxtaposition between providing professional support based on experience, knowledge and skills while enabling service users to identify their own individual strengths and solutions ideologically challenges the core purpose of social work in a personalisation context. Given this inherent dilemma, how can social workers and social work students prepare for and improve their practice within a personalisation context?

The key to this may lie in a basic social work skill that is often forgotten or overlooked by the busy professional immersed in the process-driven, performance-managed bureaucracy of their agency – listening.

Instead of using information provided by or about service users to aid the social worker in moving towards a solution, it may be more important and useful to focus on the messages beneath the surface. The skill then becomes learning how to listen and interpret rather than learning how to respond and advise. The remainder of this chapter seeks to embrace this approach. By listening to the experiences of individuals we will begin to appreciate the uniqueness of each scenario and develop skills in responding to the individual rather than the situation or information they provide.

The scenarios come from three individuals who have agreed to share information about their lives with the hope and belief that it will support your learning. The individuals have all been asked the following two questions.

1. What difference has personalisation made to you?

2. How can social workers support you in this process?

By using two open-ended questions, it is hoped that the individuals felt able to express the breadth of their experience in a way they were comfortable with. Atkinson (1998) suggests life-story interviewers need to use an informal approach using open-ended questions which help the person create and convey his or her meaning through the story. This approach also enables the individuals to emphasise key points and highlight the order and importance of any aspects of the process. In this sense the three interviews were semi-structured, allowing the interviewer to ask additional questions or seek clarification on certain points. Atkinson (1998) stresses the importance of enabling the respondent to maintain control over what goes into the story, how it is said and how it is read at the end. Atkinson asserts that giving less structure to the format of the interview will make this more likely. The interviews were recorded by hand and written up by the interviewer. The individuals were given an opportunity to make any changes before providing final approval of the written narratives. The individuals have chosen to change their names for the purpose of the book.

It must be noted that there is no intention to suggest that the three individuals represent typical experiences in relation to receiving an individual budget. The process therefore is not intended to contribute or add to any valid or reliable primary research in this area. The purpose of the chapter is to provide an opportunity to develop key social work skills, including listening, understanding, interpreting and reflecting. It also encourages an appreciation of the power dynamics that exist between the service user and the professionals. Finally, it is hoped that the narratives support students in adopting an anti-discriminatory and anti-oppressive approach to their practice, as discussed in Chapter 2.

ACTIVITY **5.1**

- *In pairs, take it in turns to describe an incident or time in your life that changed you or the way you thought about things. It could be anything from a conversation you had with someone or something major like giving birth or the loss of a loved one. Explain to your partner what happened, how it felt and how it changed your outlook.*
- *Once you have heard the story, ask your partner to summarise their understanding of what this event meant to you. Try to identify any key words the person used and the central meaning or point to the story.*

COMMENT

It would be true to say that we all use stories to describe, define and construct our lives in some way. This may involve recounting a story or anecdote to a friend or reflecting on a longer period of one's life as part of a speech, for example at a wedding, a leaving do or retirement. In each scenario the importance of the story is not only in what happened but the meaning given to it either by the individuals themselves or by others hearing the story. We may have been moved by the story in this short activity or struck by the power in this simple exchange of words. The story tells us about the uniqueness of this person, yet can be shared and understood by others. A narrative can give a window into the internalised world and suggest how the individual connects with society and culture.

Narrative studies

Before considering the three service user stories, it might be useful to explore the purpose and value of narratives generally. Smith and Sparkes (2008) suggest that we organise our experiences into narratives and assign meaning to them through story-telling. In this way, *narrative helps constitute and construct our realities and modes of being* (p. 2). Because meaning is so basic to human beings, we constantly explore the meanings that make up our own and others' worlds.

Narrative analysis assumes that language conveys meaning and that how the story is told is often more important than what is said (Goodley, 2001). Goodley suggests that narrative allows researchers to explore lived experiences and preserve a sense of the individual. It is important to recognise, however, that narratives are not simply personal but are heavily influenced by the social and cultural contexts in which individuals exist. In this sense the individual understands his or her own world according to his or her past experiences.

In recent years, narrative forms of inquiry have become increasingly visible within disability studies (Goodley et al., 2004; Marks, 1999; Smith and Sparkes, 2005; Thomas, 1999; Todd, 2006). However, this has led to debate concerning the level of emphasis placed on the individual. This viewpoint is largely located within disability studies whereby the fundamental assumption is that disability is *quintessentially collective* (French and Swain, 2006). The Disabled People's Movement insists that disability is experienced through structural, environmental and attitudinal barriers that marginalise, limit and shape people's lives. There is a concern, therefore, that to pay so much attention to the individual experience perpetuates medical-model thinking in that the problem is located with the individual and there is no need therefore for society to adjust. While expressing this concern, Armstrong (2003) suggests there must also be a recognition that to deny the individual experience can equally limit our understandings and that the social model of disability relies on an understanding of both the individual and collective experiences of disablement.

Furthermore, the absence of disabled people's voices from history has increasingly been highlighted. An appreciation of the depth of the prejudice against disabled people is unlikely without a thorough understanding of their history. The documented narratives of institutional living described by Atkinson (2005) evidence the richness of knowledge one can gain from studying the lived experiences from those who have experienced history first hand. Beresford (2003) suggests that the ignorance of researchers leads to them thinking they are better 'knowers' and sources of knowledge than the people who actually experienced it or who witnessed it.

Borsay (2005) suggests that oral history is as much about survival and change as it is to attach meaning. It provides the foundation for collective empowerment and resistance. Oral histories allow us to re-examine and develop new perspectives both ideologically and practically through policy development and practice. Borsay (2005, p. 385) suggests:

> *Oral history can bring about new understandings. It can challenge assumptions, develop a fuller, more rounded and democratic account and may even transform history.*

This is of particular importance when we consider the personalisation agenda. The documentation of the diverse and creative ways that people have personalised their own support provides ideas and support to those considering the path ahead. Sharing and disseminating individual stories have been central to empowering both individuals and professionals to think creatively. The diverse ways individuals have used their budgets have encouraged service users and professionals to think in terms of solutions rather than services.

Finally, oral histories may lead to individual empowerment. Borsay (2005) suggests that telling stories can become *acts of liberation for those whose self esteem has been battered by discrimination* (p. 7). The opportunity to review one's life is important. Finnegan (1992) suggests that the telling of personal narrative can actually help people validate their lives and make sense of their various life experiences.

This brief literature review of the value of oral histories should inform your reading of the following narratives. Clearly it is important to listen to what is being said and by whom, but we must also pay attention to the underlying messages and meanings the three individuals attach to their stories. We will reflect on the storytellers' experiences of actually telling the story and consider whether this has been an empowering or useful exercise for them. Finally, we must remember that stories need to be placed within a social and cultural context. Oliver (2000) suggests insider views, though essential, must be connected to political analysis in order to bring about change. The purpose therefore of using individual stories in this chapter is to read and reflect on the diverse experiences of the individual but then to focus on any common themes in relation to histories of marginalisation, discrimination and oppression. This will provide us with the knowledge to generate and support change in the most useful way.

The service users
Eric

Eric is a 42-year-old man. He lives in his own home and has family close by. Eric has been in his own home for two years, having lived in a residential setting prior to this. Eric describes himself as having high-functioning autism, Asperger's and mental health difficulties. Eric is a very intelligent man. He has attended university and has continued to study in areas such as history, philosophy and archaeology. Eric says he does need support to help him function in life but is clear that the support must be on his terms and he requires others to understand his perspective and mindset in order for it to work successfully.

Eric's story
I have been receiving an individual budget for a year now and I have learnt so much in that time. If I was to go back to the beginning of the year I would have done things differently but I didn't know then what I now know. I don't like the fact that I have to rely on benefits but I guess I also know that doing a job will make me ill. I have lost every job I have done. It's always the same story, I work for three months and at my first appraisal I end up being sacked. This leads to my mental health deteriorating quite rapidly. I have had a number of hospital admissions as a result. My doctor has advised me not to work and that is why I need to use an individual budget to support me at present.

For me the big difference an individual budget has made is that I have more freedom to spend the money on supporting myself in a way that suits me, although it's not been easy. Prior to receiving my individual budget I got direct payments but this was difficult as money had to be spent on support hours and although I needed support from other people I also felt I could meet my support needs in other ways if I used the money more flexibly. I was told I could use the money flexibly, but for me I like rules to be clear and I did not feel comfortable spending the money 'outside the rule book'. With an individual budget you are allowed to spend the money more flexibly so it meant I could think about things such as assistive technology and educational support, which have hugely benefited my well-being.

For example, for £300 I was able to go on an organised historical trip with other people for a week. This included accommodation, food and support to visit battlefields with guided tours. The type of support offered was ideal. It took away any worry of making arrangements and decisions, it gave me a break from my routine, it relaxed me as I enjoy educational stimulation and, most importantly, the support was no different from the support anyone else on the trip received. I could not have done this trip alone so it was a perfect option.

One of the things this has taught me is that it is much better to have money from social services with no strings attached. At the beginning, my individual budget was worked out as giving me less money than a direct payment and all I could think was: surely it makes sense to take more money. I wouldn't think that now and I would advise others to avoid making the same mistake. I would take up to 25–30 per cent less money if I knew there were no strings attached.

They give you this money to empower you to go to the market and find the right support but if you can only buy one type of support then it doesn't empower you. An individual budget has helped me discover what works for me and I can't see any other way to move forward to avoid another hospital admission. It just has to be on my terms. I've also learnt that with empowerment comes responsibility. You like the nice bits but it's all the other stuff that comes with it. There are a lot of technicalities and I have often needed more advice and help on how to spend the money. It will empower you but it can be a headache.

One of the problems with the individual budget for me was the support plan. I found this very restricting. I understand that social services need to know how I am going to spend the money and the outcomes I will get but sometimes it's hard to say what outcomes you will achieve until you have achieved them. The other problem for me is that an outcome becomes a target and it puts additional stress on me and makes it less likely for me to achieve it.

For example, one of the ways I used the money was to increase the number of dishes I could cook. This was something I had identified and I was keen to do, but the social worker wanted to quantify how many new dishes I would have learnt to prepare by such a date. This just doesn't work for me. I become focused on the target, which then becomes a source of stress and I avoid preparing new meals in fear of failing to meet the target. If I am left alone to build up my repertoire of new dishes I am actually more likely to achieve the outcome and perhaps even exceed it but I can't feel like it's a test.

I think this can actually be a particular problem for people with mental health problems. I often feel social workers and professionals see me as someone they need to fix. They see the budget as helping me overcome the problems and get better. They see mental ill health as being wrong and something they need to put right. Again this is pressure. The reality is I have mental health problems and while I can be supported to reduce the factors leading up to a breakdown, I can't eliminate this altogether.

If I am seen as having learning difficulty with Asperger's, it's fine for me to be accepted with all the nuances I have. It seems everyone will work around me and do things the way I need them to be done – a bit like 'the customer is always right'. But with mental health I am expected to adapt and change the way I do things to fit in with the norm.

Why if you label me with Asperger's and I say black is white it is OK, but if I have a mental health problem you tell me it's an illusion?

Another problem with individual budgets is how you are seen by others in society. I feel it has alienated me from my friends. I know they see me as having a 'slush fund' and really socialising has stopped since I received the budget. People have been working hard for a crust and I have just been given this sum of money for doing nothing. I know that's what people think.

When I lived in a supported-living flat and my problems were very evident to anyone who met me, it was fine for my friends. They visited me in the flat and they were OK with that. They were paying for me to be disabled and I was clearly disabled. As soon as I started walking around the streets happy-go-lucky, looking as right as rain, that was not OK.

Having the individual budget does also put pressure on me to demonstrate that the money is being well spent and I also feel I should be showing signs of recovery to suggest I am making an effort and using the money well. I used to count up how much money had been spent on me but I stopped once I got to £250,000 as it seemed obscene and what's worse, at that point I was going downhill.

I feel I should contribute to society but often I just don't know how I can do this. I resent not being able to work but I also know the danger to myself and others if I do work. It's all about risk and it's heart-breaking.

I find it hard to say what a social worker can do to help as they work within very restrictive systems. They might have ideas of working with people, working on your behalf but it is always contrary to what their managers are telling them. The framework they operate in is too conservative, negative and restrictive.

On an individual level I think social workers need to take people at face value. Don't assume you know better even if the reality is that you are talking to me at a time when my mental health is poor. You need to get inside and understand me and my way of thinking. It's no good telling me I am paranoid. Think of it in terms of me not understanding the evidence I have been presented with. It's not about colluding with me or agreeing with my statements or thoughts but just trying to share my perspective at that time. Even if you think my point of view is dubious or fanciful, take time to understand the fantasy and then work with it. Once we have this dialogue, trust can build and I will be more receptive to support or thinking about things in a different way.

Social workers need to know what's not going to be changed. The fact that things go wrong for me from time to time can't be changed but we can work on the factors leading up to it so as to reduce the frequency or degree to which it happens.

Follow-up

A few days later Eric was sent a draft of the interview and was asked how he felt about telling me his story. He replied:

> *I cannot tell you how encouraged I was after we met. I am moved by the simplicity you bring to my words. It is what I'd like to say. You have said what I said and it reads to me to mean what I meant. I cannot ask for more.*

> *You [interviewer] have heard enough to note it down, the product being recognisable as what I said and perhaps more importantly what I meant. The expression of even difficult things in that way becomes the expression of experience rather than depression or moaning about it. Thanks for the opportunity to do it and say what effect doing it had. It was very positive. I hope your readers and students will benefit from it too.*

ACTIVITY 5.2

1. *Without going back to the narrative, make a list of anything you remember to be important for Eric.*
2. *How do you think Eric can stay in control of his life and become empowered?*
3. *What have been the benefits of an individual budget for Eric?*
4. *What have been the problems associated with an individual budget for Eric?*
5. *What does Eric see as society's perception of him receiving an individual budget? Read the Introduction to Chapter 2 and think about any links with Eric's narrative.*
6. *Why does Eric feel that professionals adopt a medical model when they work with him?*
7. *If you were working with Eric, what would you be thinking about in terms of your approach?*
8. *Eric highlights systems restricting the social work role. How do you think you might address this dilemma if you were working with him?*
9. *Eric talks about the stress an outcome-focused approach puts him under. How might you support Eric to develop and demonstrate outcomes within his support plan? Think about the example of preparing dishes to help you do this.*
10. *In what ways do you think Eric's history and experiences have influenced his life today?*
11. *Do you think the process of telling his story has been an empowering experience for him? If so, how? If not, why not?*
12. *Can you make any links with the theory discussed earlier in the chapter?*

COMMENT

Hopefully you will have connected with this powerful story told by Eric and have a better understanding of how the uniqueness of his own personal biography has influenced his perspective today. You may have identified some positive ways of working with Eric and, most importantly, I hope the activity will remain with you as you go out into practice and work with individuals and their families.

Andrew

Andrew is a 39-year-old man. He lives in his own home nearby to his family. Andrew has been using an individual budget for the last four years. He uses the money to employ a personal assistant for approximately 30 hours per week to support him in various aspects of daily living. Andrew has been diagnosed with Asperger's and also has cerebral palsy. Andrew lived in a residential home for a number of years until he decided to leave and live independently with support.

Andrew's story

My individual budget has helped me to get my life back. I am now living the life I imagined I would live when I was a teenager. I have my independence. I have my own home under a shared ownership scheme with a housing association. I do what I want to do when I want to do it. There are lots of things that are important to me which I am sure other people don't realise or just take for granted, such as having my own front door key, being able to lock my front door behind me and watching my TV in my lounge rather than quietly upstairs in my room so I don't wake up other residents. I don't have to worry about waking others up.

I don't have to stick to timetables like I did in the residential home. I can have my tea when I want it. I used to have a half-hour slot between 4.45 p.m. and 5.15 p.m. when I had to prepare and cook my tea, eat it and wash up. Now I have meals whenever I want and I do prefer to eat later, like I used to with my family when I was younger. I can use my kitchen whenever I want, which I couldn't do in the residential home. Flexibility – that's the key word. Sometimes I don't have my tea and might just buy something when I am out.

I have recently employed a new personal assistant (PA), which is working out really well. I don't see him as a PA, I see him as a friend. I interviewed and chose him myself and we have lots in common, we are a similar age and I get on well with him. One of the best things about my PA, Bob, is that he had no previous experience in this kind of work so he had no set ideas about supporting people with disabilities. He doesn't know the rule book and he takes his lead from me. He is a father himself and has lots of life experience. I feel comfortable to speak my mind with Bob and we work out his hours to fit both my needs and his family life. We have lots of banter which is good and I have got to know his friends who I play football with every Friday. It's a real mix with men of different ages from early 20s to one player who is 62 years old. They are a good bunch of men who have welcomed me into their group. They even helped my Nan put up a new unit when she moved house.

I've never really had friends or anyone to say *do you want to come to the pub, Andrew?* I now know a group of men who all know my name, there's lots of banter and they treat me like one of the lads. I go out for a drink with them sometimes after football and we are going out for a meal together the week before my birthday next month.

I also use my budget to pay for an IT expert, Tom, to help me with my computer. It's really important that my computer works and I get stressed if I can't use it. I have developed a good friendship with Tom and he helps me with other gadgets and DIY jobs around the house. He also stepped in to support me when my PA wasn't available for a couple of weeks. Tom has also helped me to put something back into my community. He has helped me develop a PowerPoint presentation about my individual budget which I share with others at conferences. I think it is important that I am able to contribute in this way although I am taking a break from it for a while as it can be stressful and time-consuming.

There are some things that are hard with an individual budget. I often feel there is a lot of prejudice about people being given money to spend on meeting their own needs. I think lots of people using individual budgets feel they have to justify how they are spending the money. I think it's working well for me but I also think I am in a minority. It can also be hard to find a PA. I had to do lots of interviews and even if you get a PA who is a 100 per cent match, you may still have a problem with the service provider they work for. It's sometimes hard to work out the boundaries with a PA. They spend so much time with you in your own home and you get to know them well. Sometimes this leads to staff becoming institutionalised even when there are just two of you. It's important to feel comfortable with each other but you have to also feel you are directing the support and making the choices about what you want to do and how you want to be supported. I'm lucky because I have a good PA and I also have family to keep an eye out and help me manage the support but I do worry that if you don't get the right person and you are vulnerable and without family and friends to support you, it could go very wrong.

I don't have that much contact with my social worker as my mum helps me sort out the individual budget. I used to have weekly contact with the social worker when I was living in the residential home and it was very stressful for me and my mum. The social worker also came when there was a crisis and this happened on a regular basis.

I think it is important that social workers are honest and open. They need to be able to listen – and I mean really listen. It's important that they write down your wishes and don't just listen to what you say and then go away and do something different. I have spoken to lots of social workers at conferences and they are often very blinkered and seem a bit institutionalised. I think lots of social workers start off thinking they want to change things but then get locked into the system that doesn't let them have much freedom to do things differently.

I also think service providers find it hard to do things differently. I have met lots of individuals from service provider agencies who want to change things and tailor support to the individual but I don't believe I will see a service provider in my lifetime that can do this. They often talk the talk but then managers want them to do things a certain way and they get used to working within a system.

ACTIVITY 5.3

1. *Without going back to the narrative, make a list of anything you remember to be important for Andrew.*
2. *Try to identify some of the ways Andrew's individual budget has enabled him to become more included within his community.*

3. *Make a list of the benefits and drawbacks of receiving an individual budget from Andrew's perspective.*
4. *Andrew talks about professional boundaries and the danger of staff becoming institutionalised when working in this way. What do you think Andrew means by this?*
5. *What does Andrew value in a social worker?*
6. *What challenges does Andrew think social workers face?*
7. *Why might Andrew think that he will never see a service provider in his lifetime that can tailor support to the individual's needs?*
8. *Do you think the process of telling his story has been an empowering experience for Andrew? If so, how? If not, why not?*
9. *Can you make any links with the theory discussed earlier in the chapter?*

COMMENT

The activity should have helped you to think about some of the challenges individuals face when directing their own support. Andrew's story tells us of the positive and negative aspects. Like Eric, Andrew also talks about the prejudice individuals face in using individual budgets. As social workers it is important to recognise and acknowledge the emotional impact this process has on individuals and to support them in working through these issues.

Elizabeth (Andrew's mum)

Andrew's individual budget has been life-changing. When he was in the residential home I was in constant fear for his life. The anguish and pain of seeing your loved one suffer and not knowing what to do to make it better is terrible. It wasn't the answer to just bring him back home as this would not have given him the independence he so much strived for. He would not have the quality of life or reached his potential, as he now has. When Andrew moved into the home, we were assured that this was a move to help him become more independent and the next step would be his own home. Andrew had really wanted more independence and was troubled by his inability to get this prior to moving into the residential home. I worried about every phone call and I could not believe the decline I saw in Andrew in such a short space of time. Towards the end of his time in the residential home, Andrew was heavily medicated, had put on a lot of weight and was a shadow of his former self. When I look at him today I can hardly believe the difference.

During his time in the residential home, I had often thought how I could use **the** money spent on him in the home to plan a better life for him living independently but just assumed this was not possible within the rules. Then I read a book by Simon Duffy called *Keys to citizenship*. I couldn't believe I was reading something that I had thought about and I was convinced this would be right for Andrew. I took the book to social services and waved it in front of them as I knew they wouldn't believe me.

At first I felt like I did a lot of shouting and had to make people listen but we did have a good social worker who listened to our side of the story and eventually saw that the residential home was not right for Andrew. The social worker learnt with us about individual budgets and a pilot scheme allowed us to eventually set one up. Once the light went on for us as a family, as well as the social worker, he was brilliant and I really believe he felt proud of what he helped us achieve. He did things that had not been done before, and helped Andrew individually and imaginatively, always taking the lead from Andrew. It certainly was a steep learning curve for both him and ourselves but it was worth it.

Andrew is back to himself, absolutely himself. He is happy, he's getting pleasure from life and he's at peace. He has fun in life and also contributes to society in telling his story and helping to train staff. I still get a kick out of seeing how well he is doing. I often go home and tell my husband something he has achieved and I can't quite believe it when I think back to the days in the residential home. I would never have believed Andrew could be living the life he lives today. He is in good physical shape and is on no medication. He has no issues with obsessive-compulsive disorders which were a real problem for him.

I really believe that it was purely the environment that led to Andrew's decline. When you take away a person's life so they have no control over it, no say in what happens, they become so isolated. It's like torture. Andrew had no reason for living. Everything was controlled and we just couldn't see a way out. He had so many labels attributed to him such as 'high complex needs', 'difficult to handle' and 'attention-seeking', none of which are the real Andrew. Now he is just Andrew. And he has got rid of the labels.

Social workers really need to listen to individuals. They mustn't arrive with their own agenda with what's going on in the office. They need to put the person in the centre. Social workers must believe in themselves and stand firm in their beliefs and values. They must not be swayed by other agendas such as management issues and resource issues. Once they start doing this, they lose sight of the person being at the centre. They need to dig their heels in and stand firm. They should think about the individual as if they were their own. That doesn't mean crossing boundaries or becoming unprofessional, but just adopting the mindset, 'would this be OK for my grandmother?'

Looking back on Andrew's life it is like watching a picture or a film and seeing how things have evolved. We have come a long way and it's been a steep learning curve but I feel we have achieved change for Andrew and for others, which does give some satisfaction. Looking back now and talking about it again makes me realise just how far he has come and how brilliantly well he is doing.

ACTIVITY 5.4

1. *Without going back to the narrative, make a list of some of the words Elizabeth used to describe the transition Andrew has made.*
2. *Elizabeth describes putting trust in professionals who had suggested residential care would be right for her son. How do you think this made her feel towards those professionals when she saw Andrew's decline?*

3. What factors did Elizabeth attribute to her son's decline?
4. What challenges did Elizabeth face when trying to get the best for her son?
5. Elizabeth describes the constant use of negative labels. How do you think this impacted on Andrew and his family?
6. In what ways does Elizabeth believe social workers can support individuals and their families?
7. Do you think the process of telling her story has been an empowering experience? If so, how? If not, why not?
8. Can you make any links with the theory discussed earlier in the chapter?

COMMENT

This activity demonstrates the impact on the wider family. Elizabeth describes her frustration and clearly felt her views and ideas would not be valued. It is interesting to note that she had a clear vision for Andrew but felt unable to convey this to the professionals until she had a book to prove it (Duffy, 2003). As social workers it is important to remember that expertise can often be found within the individual and their family. The role of the social worker is to help release the imagination that individuals have and value their contribution. It is also interesting to note that although Elizabeth was always willing to work with professionals, she often felt she needed to be very assertive and forthright in getting the best support for her son.

ACTIVITY 5.5

Hopefully the three narratives have helped you to think about some of the benefits and drawbacks of receiving an individual budget. You may also have made some links with the theory both in this chapter and in Chapter 2. To help you reflect on these narratives think about and discuss with others the following questions.

1. Were there any similarities in the experiences or viewpoints for the three individuals? If so, what were they and why do you think these were shared values?
2. Were there any differences in the three narratives? If so, what were they and why might there have been diversity in their values or perspectives?
3. In what ways might narratives help you to develop good practice within social work?

COMMENT

Narratives give us some additional insight into the internal worlds of others. The three individuals describe experiences and events which have shaped their lives. They have also attached meaning to those experiences which help us to understand how they relate to society, and in this case professionals. Their past experiences and histories have clearly influenced their interpretation of events and in both cases the experience of making a transition from residential care to independent living and gaining control in their lives is

(Continued)

(Continued)

a shared value upon which they all place great importance. There are many differences in the way Eric and Andrew have designed and directed the support in their life and they differ in the emphasis they place on certain aspects. For example, Eric describes the process of support planning and needing to be in complete control as crucially important, whereas Andrew emphasises the importance of relationships and extending social networks as centrally important.

All three value social workers who can listen and try to understand their perspective. They also share in their belief that social workers have to be strong and committed to work within very challenging and restrictive organisations.

RESEARCH SUMMARY

The SCIE published a literature-informed discussion paper in 2007 (Shaping Our Lives et al., 2007). Lead author Peter Beresford used the paper to highlight the experience and views of service users and carers as part of the wider national review of social work practice in England. In light of major policy changes and direction in social work including the personalisation agenda, the research focused on the activities and tasks social workers engage in and the approach and qualities social workers possess. The following findings emerged.

- *Service users placed a particular value on the social work relationship and positive personal qualities such as warmth, respect, being non-judgemental, listening, treating people equally, being trustworthy, openness and honesty, reliability and communicating well.*
- *Service users value social work practitioners who:*
    - *support them to work out their own agendas with them;*
    - *give them time to sort things out;*
    - *are available and accessible;*
    - *provide continuity of support;*
    - *are reliable and deliver;*
    - *are responsive;*
    - *have a good level of knowledge and expertise;*
    - *value the expertise of the service user.*

In relation to self-directed support, service users and carers reported traditional professional approaches to assessment as being particularly unhelpful. Service users wanted to see social workers drawing on principles of independent living and rights-based approaches in supporting them to make their own self assessment.

COMMENT

It is interesting to note that many of the attributes and approaches highlighted in this research were mentioned by Eric, Andrew and Elizabeth. All three narratives identified the importance of working from the service user's agenda rather than organisational priorities. High value was placed on basic social work skills such as listening, respect, openness and good communication. While the research paper highlights the importance of the social work role, service users and carers clearly articulated the need for their own expertise to be acknowledged, valued and used in developing appropriate support and solutions.

CHAPTER SUMMARY

This chapter has provided an insight into the experiences of three individuals directing their own support. While these experiences cannot be generalised, they offer a chance to consider the potential opportunities and barriers involved in supporting people to direct their own support. The narratives encourage the reader to develop reflective practice by taking time to listen to and understand service users' perceptions of events and experiences. Practitioners can support service users to identify their own solutions rather than being too quick to jump in with standard service responses. The chapter has helped you to make important links between theoretical perspectives and practice. The chapter has encouraged the reader to consider the ethical principles and dilemmas involved in balancing the importance of the individual perspective versus the collective experience of disability.

It would appear from both the narratives and the research findings above, that while roles, tasks and approaches are changing, service users and carers remain unchanged in their expectation that personal qualities such as warmth, respect and openness are integral to all social work practice.

FURTHER READING

Atkinson, D (2004) Research and empowerment: Involving people with learning difficulties in oral and life history research. *Disability and Society*, 19 (7), December: 691–703.

This article draws from two oral and life-history projects to explore the multiple uses of storytelling. It focuses on learning disability and the reader is encouraged to develop insight into the meaning of people's past experiences.

Atkinson, D (2005) Narratives and people with learning disabilities, in Grant, G, Goward, P, Richardson, M and Ramcharan, P (eds) *Learning disability: A life cycle approach to valuing people.* Berkshire: Open University Press. Chapter 1, pp. 7–27.

This chapter provides a number of narratives from people with learning disabilities who have lived in institutional settings. The reader is encouraged to understand their histories and transitions following the closure of such institutions, exploring how they adapted to living in the community.

www.scie.org.uk/socialcaretv

You can watch a number of videos documenting personal stories from individuals who are directing their own support. The series covers a range of service user groups and settings.

Chapter 6

Safeguarding and personalisation

David Gaylard

Introduction

This chapter explores the association between adult safeguarding and personalisation in practice. Adults can often become eligible for community care support due to a multitude of factors, e.g. physical, social, environmental reasons, coupled with particular needs including old age, physical and/or mental health needs, or disabilities. It is often a combination of socio-economic and environmental factors, such as poor housing, poverty, poor social support networks, and an inability to work, that may result in further isolation and exclusion from society which often compounds these complex issues and creates levels of dependency that may require social work assessment and intervention. It is these complex layers of dependency, where all these issues intersect, that can on occasions expose adults to heightened level of risk which can result in some cases in subsequent harm, abuse or exploitation.

Safeguarding adults policy overview

The focus of this chapter does not allow sufficient depth to extensively explore the current adult safeguarding policy context. Greater critical analysis is provided by more applied texts such as Mandelstam (2013), Scragg and Mantell (2011) and Pritchard (2009). However, a brief contextual overview is helpful if readers are unfamiliar with the piecemeal nature of adult safeguarding policy that has evolved within the UK (separate from Scotland). For an in-depth discussion of the Scottish (Adult Protection) legislative framework, refer to Fennell (2011) and Chapter 4 in Scragg and Mantell (2011).

Key statutory guidance in England commenced with *No secrets: Guidance on developing multi-agency policies and procedures to protect vulnerable adults from abuse* (DH, 2000). In addition, *Safeguarding adults* (ADASS, 2005) provided a safeguarding good practice framework used by many local authorities. Among other things, multi-agency arrangements have been influenced by the Dignity in Care campaign, equalities and human rights legislation, Fair Access to Care Services (FACS) guidance, mental health legislation and wider debates about safeguarding children systems. All support for decision-making in relation to self-directed support should be in line with the principles of the Mental Capacity Act 2005.

In 2000, the Welsh government issued strategic guidance to authorities in Wales called *In safe hands*, with the aim of tackling adult abuse. It established the national framework for the development of local policies, procedures and guidance for the protection of vulnerable adults. *In safe hands* provided social services departments with the lead co-ordinating role with a range of partners including the NHS and police. Duties included developing and implementing local arrangements to prevent, identify, respond to and prevent abuse of adults in all settings and to take appropriate action against perpetrators of abuse. In 2010, an independent review of *In safe hands* was commissioned by the Welsh Assembly government. Researchers were asked to look specifically at adult protection with a view to recommending the need for new legislation. An Adult Protection Project Board was established to review the Welsh government adult protection policies and guidance and to make recommendations to Welsh ministers.

In 2009, the Department of Health undertook an extensive review of *No secrets*, consulting with key stakeholders involving 12,000 participants, plus 3,000 citizens to whom guidance was relevant. Despite the evidence and support for legislation (advocating for similar powers outlined in the Adult Support and Protection (Scotland) Act 2007), the Coalition government has not yet committed to give any parliamentary time to such new legislation – so there appears to be little political desire to grant parliamentary time for safeguarding adult legislative reform. The *No secrets review* (DH, 2009b) did reinforce the importance of empowerment as a fundamental building block to safeguarding, and that safeguarding decisions should be taken by the individual concerned, while being supported to retain control and make their own choices.

More recently, the Protection of Freedoms Act 2012 (enacted in September 2012) created the Disclosure and Barring Service (DBS), which became operational from December 2012. It has since merged the Criminal Records Bureau (CRB) and Independent Safeguarding Authority (ISA) functions to form a new, streamlined body providing a proportionate barring and criminal records check. Its primary role is to help employers in England and Wales make safer recruitment decisions, so preventing unsuitable people working with vulnerable groups including children. A similar scheme, 'Disclosure Scotland', covers Scotland.

The DBS statutory responsibilities are to process criminal record checks, decide whether it is appropriate for a person to be placed in or removed from a 'barred list', and maintain both the Children's and Adult's Barred list. From 2013–14, a single disclosure certificate will be issued only to the individual. It will be made a legal requirement for all employers to check whether a person is barred prior to employing them in a 'regulated activity' such as social work, healthcare, personal and social care work.

Putting policy into practice

All adults are entitled to live in a manner they wish and to accept or refuse support, assistance or protection as long as they do not harm others and are capable of making decisions about these matters.

(McKenzie, 2000, p. 9)

Therefore, all adults should receive the most effective, but *least restrictive and intrusive* form of support, assistance or protection when they are unable to care for themselves or their assets.

The *least restrictive and intrusive* principles are key intervention values enshrined in the Mental Health Act 2007 and the Human Rights Act 1998, and remain fundamental social work values underpinned in the Health and Care Professions Council (HCPC) Standards of Proficiency (e.g. Standard 6: be able to practise in a non-discriminatory manner – HCPC, 2012) and HCPC Guidance on Conduct and Ethics for Students, and the British Association of Social Workers Code of Ethics: Statement of Principles (BASW, 2012) respecting the right to self-determination, challenging unjust policies and practices, and assessing and managing risk.

Practitioners must bear these fundamental principles in mind with regard to adult safeguarding practices. All key statutory agencies need to ensure that their responses are proportionate to the level of concern and risk.

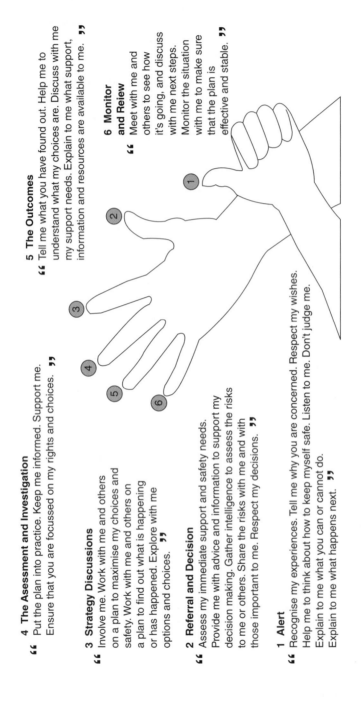

4 The Assessment and Investigation

❝ Put the plan into practice. Keep me informed. Support me.
Ensure that you are focussed on my rights and choices. ❞

3 Strategy Discussions

❝ Involve me. Work with me and others
on a plan to maximise my choices and
safety. Work with me and others on
a plan to find out what is happening
or has happened. Explore with me
options and choices. ❞

2 Referral and Decision

❝ Assess my immediate support and safety needs.
Provide me with advice and information to support my
decision making. Gather intelligence to assess the risks
to me or others. Share the risks with me and with
those important to me. Respect my decisions. ❞

1 Alert

❝ Recognise my experiences. Tell me why you are concerned. Respect my wishes.
Help me to think about how to keep myself safe. Listen to me. Don't judge me.
Explain to me what you can or cannot do.
Explain to me what happens next. ❞

5 The Outcomes

❝ Tell me what you have found out. Help me to
understand what my choices are. Discuss with me
my support needs. Explain to me what support,
information and resources are available to me. ❞

**6 Monitor
and Reiew**

❝ Meet with me and
others to see how
it's going, and discuss
with me next steps.
Monitor the situation
with me to make sure
that the plan is
effective and stable. ❞

Figure 6.1 Personalised safeguarding responses

(Making Connections (Isle of Wight) Ltd, 2011)

COMMENT

Figure 6.1 provides a personalised summary showing the path an adult safeguarding referral (sometimes referred to as an 'alert'), should take. It shows the key stages from a person-centred perspective and how it should be managed by the lead agency (usually the local authority statutory adult services department). This does not, of course, replace practitioners consulting with investigating managers or referring to copies of their multi-agency safeguarding adults' procedures (now accessible via local authority websites), so that practitioners also obtain detailed and specific operational practice knowledge and information.

Stevenson (1996), however, alerts us to the dangers of over-proceduralisation occurring within safeguarding adults when compared to safeguarding children. It is important to highlight that procedures alone do not always immediately assist new practitioners or managers, as they focus upon procedural guidance not on the professional skills required, e.g. local operational knowledge, practice experience, and confidence to assertively question, enquire and challenge allied professionals' assumptions or care providers with regard to capacity, risk, malpractice, poor standards of care or areas of discriminatory practice.

What does research tell us about practitioners' attitude to risk?

A constant dilemma for social workers operating within statutory practice is how to maintain a balance of the 'care versus control' scales (see Figure 6.2) by actively promoting an individual's independence and freedom while offering a degree of

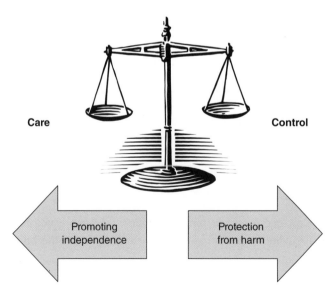

Figure 6.2 Care versus control scales

protection for the service users who may require statutory interventions or community support in line with FACS eligibility thresholds (see Chapter 3) for statutory services.

Mitchell and Glendinning (2007) undertook a UK review on risk perceptions and risk management strategies within adult social care and discovered that studies tended to concentrate on risk in relation to mental capacity, competence of people with mental health problems, physical risks for older people, competence and some positive risk-taking for people with learning disabilities. Views of people who use services were largely absent, with few evaluations of risk management systems and interventions.

Professional assumptions regarding the competence and capacity of people with mental health needs were found to be linked to the perceptions of dangerousness regarding black mental health service users. The review also highlighted that both people who use services and practitioners may withhold, or be reluctant to share, risk-related information. This can leave people without support when taking the risks that they consider important to them, or alternatively leave them poorly informed about options and choices. Other studies (examining the experiences of direct payment users) emphasised the positive benefits of the risk involved with purchasing their own care.

ACTIVITY **6.1**

Risky behaviour

Try to think about some of the risks you take in your own everyday life. It could be something like walking home alone late at night, smoking, drinking alcohol to excess, cycling (without a helmet) in a busy urban area, crossing a busy road, texting while walking, riding a motorbike or horse, or perhaps playing a contact sport such as football, rugby or hockey.

Make two lists, first noting the potential benefits involved in taking the risks, the other the dangers associated with your chosen activity.

The benefits	The dangers

Now imagine that a close friend or family member has been asked to carry out a risk assessment to decide whether you should be allowed to carry out this behaviour.

- *Do you think they would have similar lists?*
- *Do you think they would agree to the risks?*

The key theme of this activity is to demonstrate the individual nature of choice and risk. Unless we have a real appreciation of our own freedoms and choices in relation to risk, then we are not able to fully support service users effectively. Risk-taking is a unique experience – for one person perhaps a bungee or parachute jump is a risk too far; for someone else it may be their job. Our age, upbringing, social capital, personal strengths, financial situation, health, previous experiences or fears all influence how we balance risk and choice. In choosing a family member or friend to carry out a risk assessment, they may have come up with a different list from your own and the balances between the choices and risks may also be different. We have the freedom to make choices but service users often do not have complete power or freedom about major (or minor) aspects of daily living. Because money is being provided from the public purse, practitioners have power, influence and control over the decisions services users make. On occasions, practitioners may adopt defensive practices by imposing either personal (or organisational) values when working with adult service users at risk.

Risk in context

By moving to a personalised way of operating social care one is not moving from a risk-free environment in the current system or stable satisfactory position to one of full risk. Activity 6.2 illustrates how our own personal judgements can influence our perception of risk. The activity also highlights the risk attached to providing care to vulnerable people in institutional settings. Recent inquiries, such as the Mid-Staffordshire Hospital Inquiry in 2013, noted the poor Standards of care and institutional abuse taking places in institutions charged with caring for some of the most vulnerable people in our communities.

As Glasby and Littlechild (2009) highlight, new ways of working are often subject to greater scrutiny than current approaches, with the result that we criticise the new without subjecting the old to the same standards of critical scrutiny. Therefore, one should also be concerned about adults in the 'system', for instance, younger adults in care settings, those with fluctuating mental capacity or dementia in placements where inspection reports highlight dangers of isolation, maladministration of medication to the detriment of health, and difficulty of direct access to primary healthcare services.

Perceptions of safety and risk

Do you agree or disagree with the four statements below?

1 *People are safer when they live in congregated institutional care settings.*
2 *People are safer when they are in regulated services.*

(Continued)

(Continued)

3   *People are safer when they have staff who have been trained in a particular way.*
4   *People are safer when staff have DBS (Disclosure and Barring Service) checks.*

COMMENT

There are no right or wrong answers, but it may help you to consider what we mean by safety. Can an environment, inspection regime, training programme or strict monitoring guarantee absolute safety? While all four statements enhance safety for an individual, we need to be careful that we are not lulled into a false sense of achieving safety. For example, in terms of institutional living there have been numerous inquiries and serious case reviews devaluing experiences individuals have lived through, such as Beech House in 1993, Long Care, (Buckingham in 1998, Sheffield City Council in 2004, Cornwall PCT in 2006, Sutton and Merton in 2007, Winterbourne View, Castlebeck in 2011, Mid-Stafford Hospital Inquiry in 2013, and Orchid View, West Sussex in 2013.

Action on Elder Abuse (2004) found that the risk of abuse was 10 per cent higher if you live in a registered care home when compared with living at home. DBS checks tell us something about a person's criminal history but not everything about their past, and will not inform us of any recent change to that situation. The reality is that one can never be assured of complete safety, and services have never been and probably never will be completely immune from individual abusive practices.

What is risk?

Risk is the probability that an event will occur that has beneficial or harmful outcomes for a particular person or others with whom they come into contact. An event can occur because of risks associated with disability or impairment, e.g. falls. Risks can be associated with changes in relationships, e.g. isolation, loss or bereavement. Accidents can occur while in the community or within a social care setting. Risks can be associated with the activities of daily living and increased by chronic illness, disability or behaviours that could result in injury, harm, neglect, abuse or exploitation by self or others. The level of risk is often determined by the type of event and the impact of the outcome. This significantly depends on the nature of the individual, their personal resilience, their supportive relationships with others and the circumstances they find themselves in.

What should practitioners do?

The Department of Health (2010) offers some practical suggestions for practitioners to incorporate safeguarding and personalisation principles. These can be summarised as follows:

- Develop positive thinking about risk and personalisation.

- Do not assume risk based upon factors such as diagnosis or service use, but base decisions upon the individual, their circumstances, actual statements and behaviours.

- Risk assessments must remain proportionate to individual circumstances.

- Ensure that decisions regarding capacity are based upon 'best practice' principles drawn from the Mental Capacity Act 2005 codes of practice.

- Employ a strength-based perspective in your practice by focusing outcomes and solutions.

- Ensure that you are fully conversant with your local authority's safeguarding policies and procedures.

- Adopt a whole systems approach, liaising with fellow professionals from the multi-disciplinary team (where appropriate).

In essence, practitioners need to demonstrate that service users have an ability or willingness to be supported to self-care – for example, opportunities to learn new skills. Practitioners also require both the skills and the confidence to explore existing informal (or formal) networks of support. Do they exist? Can they be created to combat social exclusion and isolation? Consideration of the environment is also fundamental. Can it be adapted or improved with specialist equipment or assistive technology? Do service users and carers have the ability to identify their own risks and to find solutions? As highlighted earlier, the 'least restrictive' principles need to be considered alongside the quality of life outcomes in terms of the risk to independence of 'not doing'.

Balancing risk and safety

Having written, taught and been a practitioner in the field of adult safeguarding, I draw heavily here upon Duffy's (2006) opposing (somewhat caricature) cultural belief systems which operate within the social care system and the potential of self-directed support to develop a more positive approach to managing risk (see Table 6.1).

Interestingly, much of the debate on personalisation has centred on how well the agenda might work in different user group settings – with doubts raised as to how appropriate these ways of working may be for older people in particular. My view is that personalised approaches are crucial for all service user groups, but that it may be necessary to work differently (or harder) in some areas, due mainly to the occupational culture or history of some of these settings. What is crucial is that practitioners try to tailor support to individual circumstances, and also adapt our approach to risk and regulation on an individual basis. While some older people may hold differing approaches to certain aspects of risk than perhaps some younger individuals, we can still tailor support and regulation accordingly (and indeed it should not assume that older people will necessarily be any different from anyone else).

Table 6.1 Social care and self-directed support beliefs

Social care beliefs	Self-directed support beliefs
Disabled people are vulnerable and should be taken care of by trained professionals.	Every adult should be in control of their life (including the risks they wish to take or avoid), even if they need help with decisions.
Existing services suit people well – the challenge is to assess people and decide which service suits them.	Everybody needs support that is tailored to their situation to help them sustain and build their place in the community.
Money is not abused if it is controlled by statutory authorities or large care provider organisations.	Money is most likely to be used well when it is controlled by the person or by people who really care about the person.
Family and friends are unreliable allies for disabled people and should be replaced by independent professionals.	Family and friends can be the most important allies for disabled people and make a positive contribution to their lives.

(Adapted from Duffy, 2006, p. 10)

CASE STUDY

Personalisation and safeguarding

Grace is a frail 66-year-old African-Caribbean, wheel-chair user, insulin-controlled diabetic with MS who lives on the outskirts of a market town in a rural area of Sussex. Grace transferred her community homecare support package (previously provided by her local authority) over to an individual budget scheme following encouragement by her social worker 12 months ago after successfully recruiting a couple of personal assistants (PAs) from her local village. Grace noted an improved flexible responsive service which met her variable needs after she was able to manage her own care service needs.

However, Grace has since contacted the Adult Help Desk to express concerns that her main PA (Lisa) arrived for an evening shift smelling of alcohol and drunk. Until that point Lisa had been a reliable PA. Grace explained that Lisa had been drinking due to 'domestic pressures'. Although Grace wanted to give Lisa 'the benefit of the doubt', it soon became apparent that Lisa was so drunk it would be dangerous for her to assist Grace in getting into bed. When Grace tried to send her away Lisa became verbally abusive, refusing to leave and demanding immediate payment for her week's work. Grace then tried to phone a friend, but Lisa tried to grab the phone from her. It was only after Grace's friend called the police that Lisa eventually left.

- *What risk(s) can be identified from this case study?*
- *What role, if any, should a social worker have in this situation?*
- *What advice and guidance might Grace need to consider in terms of her future employment of PAs?*
- *What contractual employment clauses (or safeguards) might Grace revise in light of her experiences with Lisa?*

COMMENT

This case study and the research summary below both highlight the need for Grace's situation to be viewed as a safeguarding matter, so that an 'alert', can be raised with the local authority where Grace resides. This should result in an initial (but proportionate) investigation involving Grace. Lisa may well be working with other isolated adults in the community or undertaking agency social care work elsewhere. Besides her 'domestic pressures', Lisa could have alcohol dependency needs which may require her to seek help. Lisa's drinking could potentially place other service users (not to mention herself) at risk regarding lifting and handling or personal care tasks.

Some service users often seek both character checks and employment history references for up to a five-year period or more, while some may also seek a DBS check. There does, however, remain some resistance from some disability groups towards seeking DBS checks for PAs, as this is viewed as a retrograde drift back towards regulated care and indicate a lack of clarity regarding where responsibility for safeguarding against financial abuse rests (Gilbert and Powell, 2011). In addition, some user-led organisations and advocacy groups (e.g. Independent Living Association) provide services to those contemplating self-directed support, in terms of helping with advertising, recruiting and selection of PAs and guidance so that important contractual employment safeguards (e.g. holiday, sickness, dismissal) are put in place from the initial recruitment phase and beyond.

RESEARCH SUMMARY

Flynn's (2006) study, Developing the role of personal assistants, consisted of 16 participants comprising: people who had physical disabilities (one of whom was an older person), people with complex needs including learning disabilities (two of whom were young people), two people who had mental health needs, and two older people. Of the 16 participants, four were from BME communities where English was not their first language. Of the 14 personal assistants (PAs) interviewed, 12 were women (including a mother of a person receiving direct payments) and two were men. Six of the interviews were carried out one-to-one.

Key findings

- *This study found no evidence that the support available to supplement and/or replace family care-giving before they received direct payments had been experienced as adequate. Participants gave many examples of damaging, inflexible, irrelevant and disrespectful services and so saw direct payments as having freed them from these.*

(Continued)

(Continued)

- *The work of PAs is about people skills, common sense, experiential knowledge and having the right disposition. There was considerable agreement as to the range of tasks for which assistance is required and personal qualities that are sought by service users and their families. Personal care activities, household tasks, knowledge of a person's biographical life, effective listening and communication skills, empathy, trustworthiness, sharing activities and pastimes, and personal qualities such as 'going the extra mile', were all identified.*
- *Recruitment and anxiety about getting the right PA affects people deeply. Several expressed concern about the limited employment pool from which PAs can be recruited. The longer-term implications of unregulated employment status, potential exploitation of PAs, job insecurity, working conditions, short hours, health and safety matters, and training and support were cited. These findings were echoed in subsequent research by Land and Himmelweit (2010) entitled Who cares: who pays?*
- *Support of a peer group (engaged in similar work) was not an option for most PAs who work with people who receive only a few hours of weekly support. The support of a PA peer group engaged in similar work was highly valued by service users and carers.*
- *From a safeguarding perspective, participants' reports included broken trust, dishonesty, discourtesy, incompetence and abuse: neglect, physical, sexual, financial and psychological. Half the people getting direct payments in this study described abuse they or loved ones had experienced. Safeguards included only employing people they knew well and trusted and being around when PAs were present. Significantly, no formal adult safeguard alerts had been made and no complaints or adult protection procedures invoked.*

Health and safety and duty of care implications

On occasions practitioners who adopt a risk-adverse approach quote health and safety or duty of care reservations when making risk-adverse decisions or support plans. However, the Health and Safety Executive endorses a sensible approach so that health and safety legislation does not prevent reasonable activity (DH, 2010c). Any duty of care concerns need to be balanced with the 'duty to involve' which was implemented across England in 2009. It is also important to highlight that case law tends to take a more positive and pragmatic approach to risk:

> *A sensible approach is not striving to avoid all risk … [it aims] in particular to achieve the vital good of … personal happiness. What good is making someone safer if it merely makes them miserable?*

> (Justice Munby in DH, 2010c)

The case study of Ethel illustrates Justice Munby's point further.

Ethel's risks and choices

Ethel is an 89-year-old widow who, following a fractured hip, had a long hospital recovery. A 'ready to discharge decision', made by an orthopaedic surgeon means that she now has a choice to make, whether to accept the risk of a nursing home placement (with a view to permanency) or to return to her home environment where she lives alone, which is messy, risky and the one in which she suffered her recent fall. Given a good understanding of the risks, the choice would have been something along the lines of either a nursing home placement (option A) or a return home (option B). Let us briefly look at the possible outcomes for Ethel.

- *Option A: nursing home Ethel will be warm, fed and washed, have prescribed medication administered, and picked up if she falls, as a minimum. However, her placement is 20 miles from her home, friends and church, so people will be unable to visit her. Her GP whom she has known for 35 years will no longer be her GP.*
- *Option B: a return home Ethel would return to a familiar home environment, be in contact with her network of friends, family, church, and still see her GP and district nurse. However, she would continue to live in an untidy, risky physical environment which could not be fully mitigated by adaptations. Her rural isolation will contribute to her risk and her physical health means further falls are likely without 24-hour support and care. Ethel's dislike of technology means that a basic Telecare pendant alarm may not be a feasible option.*

COMMENT

In this (fictional) case study the multi-disciplinary hospital team decided that it was too risky for Ethel to return home (due to her poor rehabilitation potential and slow mobility). Ethel was informed that this was the case and so reluctantly accepted the decision. Ethel went to live in a nursing home, but quickly became depressed and died within six weeks of her nursing home admission, despite arriving in good health at the time.

Unfortunately, we do not know what the outcome would have been if Ethel had returned home, but those who knew her best (including her neighbours and son) knew that her own choice in relation to risk would have been to return home, lessen the risk as much as possible and live with the consequences. Living her last weeks away from her home (with strangers in a place she did not want to be) may have been her worst nightmare. It is important to acknowledge that the loss of control Ethel experienced over her life was not in keeping with her chosen lifestyle, being a private, independent and self-determined woman. Ethel's case illustrates an important practice principle that as practitioners one should never forget the rights of individuals to self-determine and choose which set of risks are preferable to them.

Positive risk-taking

As we have seen, any assessment of risk can often raise difficult questions for practitioners trying to balance empowerment alongside a duty of care. Changing this situation involves both practitioners and providers supporting people who use services to take control and safely make informed decisions. Understandably, social workers and allied health care professionals have not always been confident about sharing responsibility for risk, especially if their employing organisation does not have a clear positive risk-enablement culture when located within an increasingly litigious culture. All local authorities have multi-agency adult safeguarding procedures which provide a foundation for professional standards to be demonstrated and evidenced, which now include the support planning process. If an organisation or individual can demonstrate that their decision and the processes involved in reaching it were as a matter of fact consistent with contemporary professional practices, then they have not been negligent.

Risk is often considered in terms of danger, loss, threat, damage or injury, although in addition to potentially negative characteristics, risk-taking can have potentially positive benefits for individuals and their communities. As well as considering the dangers associated with risk, the potential benefits of risk-taking should therefore also be identified: a process that should involve the individual using the services, their families and practitioners. Therefore, positive risk-taking can be part of all the stages within the personalisation process and involves the following:

- Assume that people can make their own decisions (in accordance with the Mental Capacity Act) and support people to do so.

- Work in partnership with adults who use services, family carers and advocates and recognise their different perspectives and views.

- Develop an understanding of the responsibilities of each party.

- Help people to access opportunities and take worthwhile chances.

- Understand a person's strengths and find creative ways for people to be able to do things rather than ruling them out.

- Know what has worked (or not) in the past and where problems have arisen, and understand why.

- Support people who use services to learn from their experiences which sometimes may involve supporting short-term risks for long-term gains.

- Ensure that services promote independence not dependence.

Most important within a safeguarding context is a focus on the individual concerned defining the outcomes they want for themselves. Safeguarding within personalisation is about working with a person in their own context in order to negotiate the levels of risk enablement and safeguarding that are appropriate to them. A useful analysis of risk and personalisation can be found in Glasby's (2011) overview discussion paper on risk, regulation and personalisation, which identifies some key principles to consider regarding our own responses to personalisation and risk:

1. Risk is important – but people using services frequently perceive this in a disempowering way as something imposed upon them by the system.

2. We make people safe not by segregating them but by building their confidence and fully connecting them to their communities.

3. We reduce risk if we identify risk in advance and plan what to do in an emergency.

4. We might protect people better if we could focus our safeguarding on those people who really need it.

5. Personalisation and safeguarding are (or at least should be) two sides of the same coin.

6. We set people up to fail if they do not have enough support.

Glasby (2011, p. 16) offers a cautionary conclusion by stating that the history of adult social care has been littered with projects that looked promising at the pilot stages of implementation, only to be *killed stone dead* in subsequent implementation phases. The challenge for practitioners in the current economic context is to find creative ways of working with real issues about risk and regulation without allowing this to happen again.

Risk management does not mean trying to eliminate risk entirely, as it is about being *risk aware not risk averse*. It means managing risk to maximise people's choice and control and empowering people to make decisions that others may disagree with. If the outcomes are part of the support plan and all risks have been fully discussed, understood and documented, this can lead to a better quality of life for the individual.

Fundamentally, social workers require a good understanding of how to explain the decisions they reach (within the personalisation process) but also an ability to demonstrate that their professional decisions and reasoning are defensible. Some key questions need be considered:

• Have all reasonable steps been taken to avoid harm?

• Have reliable up-to-date assessment methods been used?

• Have the correct policies and procedures been followed and documented?

Adopting a person-centred approach to risk

Independence, choice and risk (DH, 2007) offers supported decision-making questions for consideration by local authorities and practitioners when working with adults at

Table 6.2 Supported decision-making questions

What is important to and for you in your life?	Is the risk present wherever you live?
What is working well? What isn't working so well?	What do you need to do?
What could make it better?	What do staff or organisations need to change?
What things are difficult for you?	What could family, carers or PAs do?
Describe how they affect you living.	Who is important to you and what do they think?
What would make things better for you?	Are there any differences of opinion between you and the people important to you?
What is stopping you from doing what you want to do?	What would help to resolve this? Who might be able to help?
Do you think there are any risks?	What could practitioners do to support you?
Could things be done in a different way, which might reduce the risks?	How would you like your support plan to be changed to meet your outcomes?
What would you do differently?	Agreed next steps – who will do what?

potential risk. These are best gathered via a face-to-face dialogue, ideally over a period of a few meetings. The supported decision-making tool includes a checklist of questions (see Table 6.2) to aid and inform decision-making regarding independence, choice and risks between those who require services and the local authority.

In addition, numerous tools are available to support person-centred thinking, some of which originate from Smull and Sanderson's (2005) *Essential lifestyle planning* approach, while others come from person-centred approaches to risk devised by Duffy and Kinsella (Kinsella, 2000).

Some practitioners who remained unsatisfied with the repertoire of risk management tools began to devise and recombine person-centred tools in innovative and creative ways, applying them to thinking, acting and learning around real risk scenarios. The learning from this experience, reflection and discussion was refined into a process that can be applied constructively to different risk situations, bringing together people who use services and the people who care or know about them most to think about how they wish to move forward and the risks involved; making decisions, taking actions and learning together. This process is called a *person-centred approach to risk*, as devised by Allen et al. (2008), and summarised in Figure 6.3.

Bates and Silberman (2007) believe that a truly person-centred approach to risk needs to fulfil the following criteria:

- *Involvement of service users and relatives in risk assessment* Involving the person concerned and the people that genuinely care about them is one of the most fundamental tenets of any person-centred approach.

- *Positive and informed risk-taking process* This is based upon finding creative solutions rather than simply ruling things out. Such a process is built around a positive view of the person – seeking to learn what the person's skills (strengths) are, what people admire about them, as well as investigating what would be necessary to keep them safe while taking the risk.

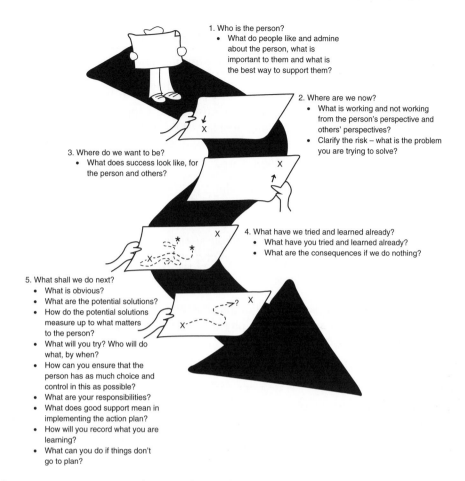

1. Who is the person?
   • What do people like and admine about the person, what is important to them and what is the best way to support them?

2. Where are we now?
   • What is working and not working from the person's perspective and others' perspectives?
   • Clarify the risk – what is the problem you are trying to solve?

3. Where do we want to be?
   • What does success look like, for the person and others?

4. What have we tried and learned already?
   • What have you tried and learned already?
   • What are the consequences if we do nothing?

5. What shall we do next?
   • What is obvious?
   • What are the potential solutions?
   • How do the potential solutions measure up to what matters to the person?
   • What will you try? Who will do what, by when?
   • How can you ensure that the person has as much choice and control in this as possible?
   • What are your responsibilities?
   • What does good support mean in implementing the action plan?
   • How will you record what you are learning?
   • What can you do if things don't go to plan?

Figure 6.3 A person-centred approach to risk

- *Proportionality* The management of the risk must match the gravity of potential harm. The least restrictive and intrusive principles remain key intervention values, as highlighted earlier in this chapter.

- *Defensive decision-making* Is there an explicit justifiable rationale for the risk management decisions?

- *Contextualising behaviour* Why did the person behave in this way? At this time, duration and in this given situation? Any contributory factors?

- *Learning* Adopting culture positive and productive approaches to risk require a deep emphasis within our ongoing learning. For example, use of learning/reflective tools, asking what is working and what is not working?

- *Identifying tolerable risks* Use creative (lateral) thinking to mitigate the risk which improve quality of life, e.g. moving from situations which make person happy but unsafe to where the person is safer, and from strategies where the person is safe but unhappy (e.g. the Ethel case study), to where they can be happier.

Safeguarding and personalisation in practice

There still appear to be difficulties for some practitioners in balancing their duty towards protection and well-being of service users and support of user choice. For many the anxiety around promoting and enabling choices that may involve risk is that they fear the consequences (e.g. Clark and Spafford, 2001; Ellis, 2007; Henwood and Hudson, 2007; Glendinning et al., 2008; Carr 2011).

A review of risk and adult social care covering 2007–12 (Mitchell et al., 2012, p. 33) concluded that:

> Overall there appears to be widespread uncertainty and a lack of evidence in how professionals can best support different groups of service users in positive risk taking.

In practice, the delivery of personalisation has been more successful with some adult service user groups, such as those with physical disabilities than, for example, those with dementia (Kinnaird, 2010).

ACTIVITY 6.3

- *Why does the uptake of personal budgets by people with dementia remain so low?*
- *To what extent do future developments regarding the personalisation of community care services give rise to greater safeguarding concerns?*

COMMENT

Moore and Jones (2012) argue that practitioners have not been promoting self-directed support in the mistaken assumption that people with dementia do not have the interest or ability to go through the process. They similarly found that people with dementia and their families also had concerns that the process would be too complicated and bureau-cratic. Lightfoot (2010, cited in Moore and Jones, 2012) found that some practitioners were not aware that if a person lacked capacity to manage their budget a suitable person such as a family member could be appointed. These examples may illustrate risk-averse behaviour by some practitioners; risk-averse behaviour informed by incorrect information or stereotypical assumptions about people with dementia. The benefits of personal budgets, particularly in terms of the flexibility that they can offer, can be significant in situations where needs may change rapidly and crises occur. However, they are also beneficial in terms of ensuring that people who are attending to intimate personal care are people you choose. As a family carer for someone with dementia said: I now have control over who comes through my door (p. 73).

In terms of risk factors and individuals' well-being, surely that should not be too much to ask?

Despite cultural and operational challenges some innovative changes have been made in terms of personalisation and safeguarding practices as illustrated by the following examples.

Community awareness and prevention

As increasing amounts of care are likely to be provided informally under personalisation the community's role in safeguarding will increase. Many PCTs and local authorities run collaborative regional campaigns or roadshow events raising the profile of adult safeguarding to encourage the public in greater reporting of safeguarding concerns to enable early intervention. These campaigns focus upon alerting members of the community to common signs of abuse or neglect, ranging from postal and other delivery workers, community wardens, high street banking staff, supermarket personnel who deliver groceries to isolated, housebound individuals dependent upon internet shopping, churches and regional charities, to user-led organisations such as Mind, Age UK and Scope.

Simplified procedures

Guidance from the Association of Directors of Adult Social Services (ADASS, 2005) recommended an eight-step procedure for handling adult safeguarding cases. Stages include alerts of possible abuse, deciding whether or not a safeguarding enquiry is necessary, formulating a plan for assessing risk, carrying out the assessment, drawing up a plan for tackling any risks identified, reviewing the plan, and recording outcomes. This can make safeguarding a separate, fragmented process, outside social workers' normal working practice in a personalised environment, although the Royal Borough of Kingston, London, for example, has since condensed its safeguarding procedures into just four stages: alert, strategy, case conference and review. The idea is that if you align the practice so that it is uniform and familiar for practitioners, they are more likely to be able to get on with it. This fits with the personalised way of working alongside service users, which is about getting to know the person and assessing their needs, planning and reviewing care. It is hoped that these moves will lead to a better experience of the safeguarding system for adults deemed at risk.

Pre-paid cards

Barking and Dagenham Council in London developed plans for a pre-payment card for those receiving personal budgets. Funding is transferred onto the card, then used to pay for care. The council believes that this provides a way to empower those who may be subject to potential financial abuse by setting up a payment system so that any alleged perpetrator does not have access. The intention is that most PAs and care providers will be paid by direct debit. Also, in the event of abuse, it ensures an audit trail that is readily accessible by the authority, allowing them to step in quickly. The scheme is managed by an external financial service partner.

Lone appointments

Speaking to service users on their own can sometimes uncover latent safeguarding concerns, which might not be voiced when a carer is present for fear of embarrassment, intimidation or repercussions. Many authorities now include lone appointments as part of its standard operating procedures for social workers.

Risk enablement

Risk enablement needs to be a core part of the self-directed support process, and personalisation and adult safeguarding practice and policy need to be more closely aligned and inform each other. They should be underpinned by the principles of person-centred practice, the promotion of choice, control, independent living, autonomy and staying safe. A shared adult personalisation and safeguarding framework can support this.

Risk enablement panels are beginning to emerge in some local authorities as a way of helping with challenging or complex decisions which may arise as part of signing off a person's support plan. This demonstrates how local authorities can implement self-directed support and personal budgets in ways that empower individuals while ensuring risks are managed and responsibility is clear. The emphasis is on shared decision-making, which supports person-centred front line practice and improves practitioner confidence. Duty of care decisions can be made in a shared and informed way, with transparent, shared responsibility.

CHAPTER SUMMARY

Personalisation has undoubtedly resulted in significant benefits and improved quality of life outcomes for many adult users, but there does remain a question about the impact in the longer term in relation to specific adult user groups currently under-represented in uptake of personalised services.

This chapter has explored the changing arena of adult social care, focusing on the delicate balance between empowering people through personalised support while keeping them safe. It has examined current adult safeguarding policy, practice and applied research. We have also critically evaluated the nature of risk and the perceptions of safety, what practitioners need to contemplate when balancing risk, health and safety, and duty of care implications. Positive risk-taking strategies and the adoption of a person-centred approach to risk and some innovative practice examples have also been outlined.

Significantly, perhaps what may now need further research scrutiny is the wider implication of risk in terms of the potential adverse impact linked to inadequate resources. There is concern that the personalisation agenda will result in reduced or less appropriate provision for some individuals, as local authorities experience increasing financial restrictions, culminating in other services being reduced or closed down as personalisation is rolled out – resulting in users and carers with less choice. Some of these relate to risk to the individual from inadequate provision, if personal budgets and direct payments remain insufficient to meet the increasingly complex needs of individuals. Those who are eligible for social care (under revised Fair Access to Care eligibility thresholds) may find it increasingly difficult to purchase appropriate services with the allocated budget – an important point given current austerity pressures being experienced by social services departments across the UK.

FURTHER READING

Journal of Adult Protection (Pier Publication)

A straightforward, approachable journal full of innovative practice-based research from researchers, practitioners and commissioners which provides valuable research, critical analysis and commentary on this rapidly evolving area of policy and practice.

Hothersall, S and Maas-Lowit, M (eds) (2010) *Need, risk and protection in social work practice.* Exeter: Learning Matters.

A comprehensive text that provides a user-friendly guide to working with risk. It critically explores notions of need, vulnerability and protection and examines theoretical concepts of each before applying them to different practice scenarios e.g. disability, mental health, older people and substance misuse.

Mandelstam, M (2013) *Safeguarding adults and the law* (2nd edn). London: Jessica Kingsley.

A recently revised, comprehensive text, well written and easy to read with all up-to-date legislation. An ideal text for any manager, newly qualified practitioner, trainer or researcher in this field of social policy.

Pritchard, J (ed) (2009) *Good practice in the law and safeguarding adults.* London: Jessica Kingsley.

An accessible summary of key legislative framework, developments and best practice, relevant for most social care practitioners, researchers, educator and care providers involved in adult protection in England, Wales and Scotland.

Scragg, T and Mantell, A (eds) (2011) *Safeguarding adults in social work* (2nd edn). Exeter: Learning Matters.

A collaboratively written introductory text (now extensively revised) that guides you through key aspects of adult safeguarding. Accessible chapters examine UK and Scottish legislative policy frameworks; the Mental Capacity Act; safeguarding children; domestic violence; working with risk; and learning from serious case reviews. A popular text for students, educators and practitioners, full of reflective activities, case studies and applied research.

WEBSITES

www.pasauk.org.uk

The Practitioner Alliance for Safeguarding Adults strives through collaboration with practitioners in statutory, voluntary and private sectors to develop practice-based interventions and to generate positive outcomes in working with the adults at risk of abuse.

www.elderabuse.org.uk

Action on Elder Abuse is a national charity which aims to protect against and prevent abuse of older people. It raises awareness, promotes education, information and support for those at risk and runs a national free helpline.

Chapter 7

Preparing for practice and the Professional Capabilities Framework

Ali Gardner

This chapter will help you to develop the following capabilities from the Professional Capabilities Framework:

- **Professionalism**
  Identify and behave as a professional social worker committed to professional development.

- **Values and ethics**
  Apply social work ethical principles and values to guide professional practice.

- **Diversity**
  Recognise diversity and apply anti-discriminatory and anti-oppressive principles in practice.

- **Justice**
  Advance human rights and promote social justice and economic well-being.

- **Knowledge**
  Apply knowledge of social sciences, law and social work practice theory.

- **Judgement**
  Use judgement and authority to intervene with individuals, families and communities to promote independence, provide support and prevent harm, neglect and abuse.

- **Critical reflection and analysis**
  Apply critical reflection and analysis to inform and provide a rationale for professional decision-making.

- **Contexts and organisations**
  Engage with, inform, and adapt to changing contexts that shape practice. Operate effectively within your own organisational frameworks and contribute to the development of services and organisations. Operate effectively within multi-agency and inter-professional settings.

- **Professional leadership**
  Take responsibility for the professional learning and development of others through supervision, mentoring, assessing, research, teaching, leadership and management.

It will also introduce you to the following standards as set out in the 2008 social work subject benchmark statement.

5.5.1   **Manage problem-solving activities.**
5.5.2   **Gathering information.**
5.5.3   **Analysis and synthesis.**
5.5.4   **Intervention and evaluation.**
5.6   **Communication skills.**
5.7   **Skills in working with others.**

The new social work degree with the introduction of the Professional Capabilities Framework (PCF) provides a changing context within which social work students will learn and be assessed. The PCF was developed by the Social Work Reform Board and is now owned by the College of Social Work. It sets out consistent expectations of social workers at every stage in their career. It consists of the nine domains set out at the beginning of this chapter. The emphasis on capabilities as opposed to competencies reinforces some of the key messages underpinning the ethos of personalisation. The PCF framework recognises that students will develop capabilities rather than working towards a very prescriptive set of competencies. This can provide more space for creative learning and practice, along with more scope for capability and progression to be demonstrated in a variety of ways appropriate to the working context. By the same token it provides an opportunity to incorporate evidence, views and perspectives of individuals wider than the practice educator in the assessment of the student's development.

The intention of the PCF is to allow for a more holistic assessment of the student and qualified social worker as they progress through their training and social work career. It provides an opportunity to move beyond the dominant ideology of acquisition of technical-rational expertise in which the professional is seen to refer to a body of knowledge and technique that is to be learned and applied. Leadbeater (2004) insists that education should be a process in which the learner discovers for themselves and reflects on this process, rather than being a transfer of knowledge and skills from teacher to learner. In many ways the use of self and critical practice outlined in Chapter 2 becomes the tools that students utilise in order to understand and support the needs of others. Lester (1999) urges practitioners to develop skills in map-making rather than just map-reading in their journey of professional development. He suggests that encouraging an enquiring, critical and creative approach at the same time as meeting the demands of the knowledge or competence of the curriculum is required. In this sense, a capability framework enables students to do more than prove competence. Lester claims that proficiency at map-reading, i.e. following other people's structures, does not necessarily transfer confidence, exploration and experimentation required to map uncharted territories and redraw the maps of known ones. Furthermore, Lester believes that an education in map-reading does not guarantee development of the abilities required for map-making, and may encourage limiting beliefs that blunt them.

ACTIVITY 7.1

Think of a time at work, on placement or in education when you have faced an unfamiliar or unpredictable set of circumstances. At first you may have been unsure of how to proceed or what to say. The situation, however, requires you to take some action. In a sense you are reflecting in action as described by Schön (1986). You are quickly trying to assess the best way forward through a process of analysis, but this can be very stressful at the time as your thought processes can be challenged and interrupted by the tension and urgency of a situation. Looking back on this situation, what do you think the experience provided you with in terms of your own learning and development? Try to write down a list of any learning points, skills or qualities you developed as a result of this experience.

COMMENT

You may have focused initially on the feelings of stress and anxiety that this situation evoked for you. Hopefully you then moved on to some of the more positive consequences of facing a difficult unfamiliar situation. Perhaps you felt a sense of confidence and satisfaction that you managed a situation or 'got through it'. This may have given you renewed confidence not only in facing similar situations but also in facing unfamiliar situations in the future. Sometimes an experience in which you feel out of your depth as a social worker is one of the most useful ways of developing a sense of confidence in your own abilities. In turn this can provide you with the skills to be critical and creative in practice even in the most complex situations. In a sense this is the difference between being a map-reader and a map-maker.

Given the context of personalisation, which calls for creative person-centred practice, largely in uncharted territories, the need for map-making, I would suggest, is an essential skill for social workers. The ability to critically engage with, and sometimes reject traditional, well-mapped paternalistic models of welfare delivery underpins the role of the social worker within a personalisation context.

As social work students you will have already demonstrated capability at entry level, in each of the nine domains of the PCF in the process of applying for and being recruited on to a social work programme. You will continue to work closely with the nine domains both in your training and as a qualified social worker as part of your continuing professional development. It is important, therefore, that you develop a good understanding of these domains and consider how they can be applied in practice. We will use this chapter to explore the levels of capability that you will be focusing on as part of your training. These include:

- readiness for direct practice (to be achieved prior to your first 70-day placement);
- end of first placement;
- end of last placement.

As you progress through the PCF, your engagement with each domain will deepen and extend as you develop knowledge, skills and confidence in your practice. Remember the discussion above about moving from a map-reader to a map-maker? In the early days of your training and in preparation for practice, you are likely to spend a lot of time reading maps, and much of your learning will come from shadowing, observing others, teaching sessions and your own reading. As you embark on your first placement there will be an expectation that you will begin to develop skills in becoming a map-maker. You will be expected to start making professional judgements and managing yourself to operate in environments of uncertainty and change. The PCF, with its focus on capabilities rather than competencies, encourages a focus on *how* you practise rather than just on *what* you do as a practitioner. In order to work out how you are going to practise, you must engage with your practice at a level deeper than that of learning from others and books. You must also engage with some self-dialogue – understand who you are, what values you hold and how they may impact on your assessments, interventions and judgements. These are the essential ingredients to becoming a creative, critical and confident practitioner. The ability to move beyond map-reading to map-making is absolutely central within a personalisation context. As we discussed in Chapter 2, there is a need to move away from notions of paternalism, whereby the professional is seen as the expert with all the answers. Self-directed support requires practitioners to relinquish power and to value service users' expertise. Essentially, the role of the practitioner is to work as an enabler and facilitator in supporting people to identify their needs and design effective support to meet their self-selected outcomes. While a student's learning and engagement with the syllabus or curriculum can act as a point of reference and support in the learning process, the practitioner must be able to move beyond seeing themselves as the sole problem-solver and work with service users in more creative ways. In this sense there is no set formula that the social worker can refer to if we are to genuinely embrace the principles of personalisation and person-centred practice. Furthermore, there is a danger for service users, if practitioners convey a sense of being the capable problem-solver. For many years, disabled people have been forced into accepting the role of passive recipient, a habit which for some will be hard to break. Practitioners, therefore, need to work sensitively with service users to ensure that they can share their knowledge and expertise and use their power carefully to support service users in accessing support while promoting service users' confidence and ability to maintain control of the process. In walking this tightrope, practitioners need to become experimenters and constructors of their own practice and the theory upon which it is based, thus become proficient map-makers.

The PCF was designed to cover all aspects of social work. At times, therefore, some aspects may appear more relevant to some working contexts than others. The matrix in Table 7.1 is an attempt to interpret some of the general meanings, interpretations and applications the nine domains could have when considered within a personalisation context. The matrix also offers some ideas in terms of how you may demonstrate progression and development of your capabilities. Practice educators may find this helpful in supporting students to identify appropriate learning opportunities within their placement learning experience.

Table 7.1 Preparing for practice – PCF and personalisation context

Domain	Personalisation context
1. Professionalism Identify and behave as a professional social worker committed to professional development.	As a social worker, we need to be clear about what we mean by acting professionally. • Is professionalism solely understood in terms of what your employer expects you to do or what the legislation requires you to do? *OR* • Is it wider than this? Can a service user decide what is professional? *AND* • What about your own belief and values about what social work is? Does this inform your interpretation of how to behave professionally? Service users will be highly dependent on your support to advocate for them in making choices and enabling them to take control of their own lives. This may challenge your own understanding of behaving professionally or the expectation of your employer. As the personalisation agenda evolves, service users are choosing different unique options. At times this may not fit easily into the traditional administrative models within which you are working. You will need to balance your professional accountability to your employer in terms of policies and procedures while remaining true to the principles of personalisation that promote service user choice and control wherever possible. Sometimes you will feel torn in acting professionally. Sometimes you may have to challenge the system in order to act professionally. Your role as a social work student should be to identify and critically reflect on these experiences through supervision with your practice educator.
2. Values and ethics Apply social work ethical principles and values to guide professional practice.	As noted in Chapter 2, personalisation is about thinking and about doing. Embracing the principles and values underpinning personalisation are essential if notions of choice and control are to become more than words for service users, carers and their families. As a student you will need to identify and critically engage with ethical dilemmas that present themselves within a personalisation context. You will need to develop your skills in ethical reasoning as you balance and respect rights and entitlements of service users with bureaucratic systems that may appear inflexible and in need of change. At times this may be challenging, as government policy and organisational policies tend to readily refer to notions of choice, control and self-directed support without fully embracing them within practice delivery. As a practitioner you need to demonstrate how notions of choice, control and service user expertise are being promoted in your practice. This includes every interaction with service users and extends further than offering choice and control through a personal budget.
3. Diversity Recognise diversity and apply anti-discriminatory and anti-oppressive principles in practice.	This is central to the personalisation context. An understanding of person-centred thinking theory is required to ensure that practice is underpinned by the recognition that support and services need to be tailored to the individual needs of service users. Skills in the application of person-centred practice will be useful in recognising diversity and applying an anti-discriminatory approach. The ability to engage with individuals and their narrative rather than basing practice on information provided solely from other professionals is required to ensure that service users are central to the process. At times this will require working creatively within rigid paperwork and administrative systems which may not naturally allow for flexible approaches to support. An understanding of the experience many service users and their families have encountered over the years in accessing support is required. Sharing power and promoting service user expertise can be difficult for individuals who have not experienced this before. Finding ways of supporting individuals to make choices in their lives while feeling supported by professionals is a key part of an individual's journey to taking control in their lives. Similarly your role as a social worker within a personalisation context may involve challenging decisions or systems that fail to support the principles of self-directed support or disempower service users. As indicated by the recent Community Care Survey of Personalisation (Community Care, June 2013), many social workers admit feeling that they lack knowledge and understanding of personalisation in practice. As a student you may have opportunities to support others in their learning process and/or challenge practice that is not promoting the principles of personalisation.

Domain	Personalisation context
4. Rights, justice and economic well-being Advance human rights and promote social justice and economic well-being.	In Chapter 2 we discussed the difference between the *professional gift model* whereby individuals are viewed as passive recipients of care and the *citizenship model* based on seeing people as having rights and entitlements and contributing to society. Within a personalisation context, the principles underpinning the citizenship model and the social model of disability (see Chapter 2) are central to promoting social justice and well-being. Promoting the rights of individuals can be done at many different levels. First, it is important to have a good understanding of the law and policy relating to personalisation. In addition it is helpful to keep up to date with the emerging legislation which is likely to endorse notions of choice and control with the provision of statutory duties. Advocating for individuals through your understanding and sharing of knowledge around legislation and policy is central to promoting and advancing human rights and well-being. Advocacy at both an individual and a citizen level are key within the personalisation context as individuals become empowered to take control of the design of their own support. As well as working at an individual level to promote rights and well-being, social workers also have a role to play in organisational change. This includes sharing knowledge, shaping services/support and at times challenging current practice and attitudes. At a time of shrinking resources and changing notions of the social work role, some social workers are very suspicious of personalisation and the future of social work. It is important that you take time to understand why this might be the case and that you consider how you position yourself within this discourse. You will need to adopt a reflective and reflexive approach in your practice and supervision to explore these debates carefully and to shape your practice accordingly.
5. Knowledge Apply knowledge of social sciences, law and social work practice theory.	Knowledge is power. This is true for both service users and professionals. Your understanding of the law and policy guiding personalisation is crucial if you are to advocate effectively on behalf of service users. You also need to feel confident in this knowledge to share it with service users. In particular you should be aware of legislation relating to direct payments and emerging legislation relating to personal budgets. You should also be aware of the policy developments and political landscape in relation to personalisation dating back to *Putting people first* (HM Government, 2007). In addition you should develop a clear understanding of the historical influences shaping personalisation. In particular the Independent Living Movement and the changing shape of welfare over the years dating back to the nineteenth-century Poor Laws. Understanding how service users have been treated in society, is central to informing the basis upon which you engage with individuals and their families in current practice. Engaging with theory is central to all social work practice. Within a personalisation context a clear understanding of the social model of disability (as discussed in Chapter 2) is central to practice. Likewise, an understanding of person-centred thinking and person-centred practice (Chapter 2) will inform your practice as well as providing a practical dimension to how you can work with individuals and families to enable them to direct their own support. The website **www. helensandersonassociates.co.uk** provides a collection of tools and literature which can support your practice.
6. Critical reflection and analysis Apply critical reflection and analysis to inform and provide rationale for professional decision-making.	To work effectively within a personalisation context, social workers need to be confident and acutely aware of the values shaping their practice. As discussed in Chapter 2, personalisation is not just a different way of doing things; it is a different way of thinking about things. As you enter practice you will be expected to engage with a steep learning curve in terms of understanding the organisation, the systems, the paperwork and the team dynamics. It can be tempting and sometimes easier to fall into the organisational regime, particularly as a student with less experience and power. It is important, however, that you remember the discussion about map-reading and map-making. Personalisation calls for practitioners who can be curious and creative in their approach and at times can reject traditional models of practice. In this sense following other people's structure or relying only on reading maps may limit your own ability to develop the confidence to experiment with new ways of working in uncharted territories, i.e. becoming a map-maker. As a social work practitioner working in complex, challenging and fast-paced contexts, it is important that you create space to reflect on your practice, consider the values, theories, politics and economic influences impacting on your assessments, interventions and professional judgements.

(Continued)

Table 7.1 (Continued)

Domain	Personalisation context
7. Intervention and skills Use judgement and authority to intervene with individuals, families and communities to promote independence, provide support and prevent harm, neglect and abuse.	This is perhaps the most challenging aspect of personalisation and self-directed support. Personalisation operates on the basis of rejecting a paternalistic approach and the sense that interventions are imposed upon people. Instead, the premise for practice is that service users and their families are experts in their own lives. Using their own experience, focusing on their own objectives, individuals make decisions about the support they need and how it should be provided. The role of the social worker is to enable and facilitate this process rather than to control it. At times this will be contentious as individuals consider the balance of promoting independence and the potential risks involved. As social workers we may perceive risks in different ways from service users. Developing skills in working collaboratively with service users and their families is crucial in ensuring that the promotion of independence versus risk and harm are carefully considered and explored. Adopting a person-centred approach to positive risk-taking which places the service user at the centre of the process and focuses on developing a plan tailored to the specific risks for an individual in their particular setting is essential. As a social worker, there are key points within the self-directed support model at which we need to engage with issues concerning the balancing of independence versus risk. At the point of assessment, the role of the social worker may involve questioning or challenging the service user's assessment of risk. This ensures that discussions happen early on in the process. At the stage of support planning, careful risk management is a process the social worker can contribute to. Identification of potential risks along with an honest exchange with service users can provide an opportunity to consider alternative measures or support that allow choice and minimise risks. Personalising reviews in terms of frequency and format allows risk management to become meaningful for the service user and their support. Encouraging the service user to focus on outcomes when planning their support highlights some of the potential risks that may need to be managed in a more intensive way while acknowledging other risks that are acceptable and do not require specific safeguards. The adoption of a person-centred approach to risk management allows a more thorough proportionate response to risk as opposed to imposing more traditional, standardised, and at times inflexible, risk management tools.
8. Contexts and organisations Engage with, inform, and adapt to changing contexts that shape practice. Operate effectively within own organisational frameworks and contribute to the development of services and organisations. Operate effectively within multi-agency and inter-professional settings.	One of the most demanding roles as a social work is understanding how the organisation you are working for operates. Each organisation has its own way of doing things, some of which are explicit, others less so, and you will find them out as you progress. Researching the organisation, its management structure, its vision or objectives and principles can be undertaken before you enter the workplace. Knowledge of legislative, policy and economic influences is also key to understanding how an organisation might work along with any local factors such as community demographics or resource/staffing issues. As a social worker you need to be responsive to changes, challenges and opportunities, and working within a personalisation context is likely to offer you many experiences of this. As discussed above, the level of engagement with the personalisation agenda will vary from agency to agency. You may join a team who have embedded this approach, providing you with knowledge, skills and experience for you to draw upon. Or you may join an organisation with less experience and/or that may be less receptive to the concept of personalisation. This can feel like a lonely place and I have spoken to many students who report this experience. On the one hand you need to demonstrate that you can be a co-operative team member but on the other hand you may be frustrated or disillusioned by the lack of appetite for personalisation. It is important that you work sensitively in this situation and try to find potential allies or opportunities to share knowledge and good practice ideas. Contributing to organisations by helping them shape future practice and direction is a challenging task and one that you will continue to develop throughout your career, but providing some level of professional leadership through the exchange of knowledge and information can be achieved even on your first placement. Within a personalisation context, it is likely that you will be required to work with many professionals and agencies. Adopting a person-centred approach and ensuring that decisions and discussions take place with the individual and are shared with all relevant parties in a co-ordinated fashion is key to the self-directed model. It is important to acknowledge and avoid some of the ways in which service users can be made to feel that they are passive recipients of care:

Domain	Personalisation context
	<ul><li>meetings happening without them</li><li>meeting having to be repeated due to professionals unable to co-ordinate diaries</li><li>meetings with too many professionals with too much to say</li><li>unnecessary meetings being held with no purpose</li><li>information or decisions being presented at meetings with no prior warning</li><li>inadequate or no advocacy service provided or offered to service user.</li></ul>
9. Professional leadership Take responsibility for the professional learning and development of others through supervision, mentoring, assessing, research, teaching, leadership and management.	There are real opportunities to offer professional leadership even as a student social worker within the personalisation context. As the 2013 Community Care Survey on Personalisation suggested, many social workers in practice still feel that they have not been trained adequately on personalisation. As a student you may be able to share information from your own training at team meetings, for example, or on a one-to-one basis. Many of the social workers in practice will have trained before changes in the law and policy relating to personalisation took place. While they will need to keep up to date with changes, they may not have had the time or space to consider these changes in any real detail. Students can often play a vital role in contributing to supporting learning and development, particularly in new or emerging areas of practice such as personalisation. It is important, however, to understand why a team may be less knowledgeable or receptive to the idea of personalisation. It may be that training has just not been offered but it could be that social workers feel quite suspicious about the move towards personalisation. It is important that you talk to the manager, your supervisor and the team before you engage in supporting learning and development to make sure you approach it positively and sensitively, acknowledging the genuine concerns practitioners have. You may also be able to demonstrate professional leadership through developing awareness of personalisation with service users and their families. This could involve providing information, engaging with group discussions or presentations or creating opportunities for service users/carers to exchange their own experiences. You could also engage the wider community and other agencies in this role and consider ways of providing information about personalisation which may lead to the development of new service providers or general awareness around the changing contexts within which social care is being delivered. Networking with local agencies, including user-led organisations, and promoting the exchange of knowledge and ideas can be one of the most effective ways of moving forward in relation to the personalisation agenda.

The Health and Care Professions Council (HCPC)

As of August 2012 the HCPC is responsible for regulating social workers and social work education providers in England. The HCPC's regulatory function is to protect the public by setting professional standards of conduct and competence, and protect service users from poor practice by holding professionals to account.

The HCPC (2012) introduced the Standards of Proficiency (SoPs) for social workers. These are threshold standards for safe and effective practice and have to be met for a person to become and remain registered. The standards outline what an individual must know, understand and be able to do when they enter the register and begin practising as a social worker. It is important that you familiarise yourself with these but also consider how the SoPs map against a personalisation context. Similarly, you will need to develop your understanding of the standards of conduct, performance and ethics set by the HCPC. The standards of conduct, performance and ethics are to be adhered to by both registered social workers and those training to become a social worker. The standards of conduct, performance and ethics cover a range of aspects connected to professional practice including the manner in which you relate and communicate to service users, practitioners and other professionals, maintaining high standards of personal conduct, keeping up to date with relevant knowledge, seeking consent where appropriate and keeping accurate records. Within a personalisation context it is important that you recognise some of the tensions the standards of conduct, performance and ethics may present when balancing the rights of services users, including promoting choice and independence while ensuring that vulnerable people are not placed in situations which present unacceptable risks.

CHAPTER SUMMARY

This chapter has focused on ways in which social work students can begin to relate personalisation to their practice. The introduction of the PCF with a focus on a capability rather than a competency based assessment framework provides opportunities to embrace and develop more creative practice and ways of demonstrating progression through the PCF.

Students undertaking placements with adults face an exciting yet challenging time as legislation and policy rapidly changes, giving rise to the expression of wide-ranging views on whether personalisation provides better or worse outcomes for service users and their families. Students entering these uncertain work settings need to do so as well-informed, confident students. They must be prepared to learn from others as well as contribute to the learning and development of qualified practitioners, service users and the wider community. Each student brings a unique skill-set to their training. In order to maintain respect for the diversity and uniqueness offered by practitioners from wide-ranging backgrounds and experiences, it is important that the learning environment is responsive to individual learning needs. Guidance from the College of Social Work reinforces this message in calling for the development of creative and flexible learning opportunities that can be tailored to the individual needs of the student. In many ways this approach is reflective of the principles underlying personalisation. If students are to facilitate individuals in personalising their support, then it surely follows that, in their training, social work students need to ensure their learning is also personalised to their specific needs. There is a real danger that applying a one-size-fits-all approach to learning stifles the potential creativity and individuality of social work practitioners, and encourages a similar approach to practice. As with supporting a self-directed model of support in which service users shift from being passive recipients of care to active citizens, so too must social work students move from being passive recipients of learning to co-producers of that learning experience. In this sense social work students must reject the notion that education is something that is done to them but rather see it as something they do to themselves.

The matrix in Table 7.1 maps the nine domains of the PCF against the personalisation context. It will be useful to study the matrix before entering your placement, and return to it as you begin to undertake learning activities that can assist in demonstrating your progress.

In the next chapter a newly qualified social worker provides an insight into her learning experience in the process of training to become a social worker. Reflecting on her journey from support worker through to practitioner she provides an honest and powerful reflection of how her engagement with the values, knowledge and skills underpinning personalisation has shaped her current practice.

FURTHER
READING

Lomax, R, Jones, K, Leigh, S and Gay, C (2010) *Surviving your social work placement.* London: Palgrave Macmillan.

This book is a useful and informative guide for students undertaking practice placements. While it doesn't refer specifically to practice learning within a personalisation context, it contains a wealth of accessible information relating to the experience of learning on placement.

Parker, J (2010) *Effective practice learning in social work* (2nd edn). Exeter: Learning Matters.

This book covers all aspects of practice learning, and features a chapter on the social work value base, which links well with issues raised in this chapter. This book addresses many of the anxieties that students report, in relation to practice learning, and is therefore essential reading.

Chapter 8

Personalisation – A newly qualified perspective

Natalie Robinson

This chapter will help you to develop the following capabilities from the Professional Capabilities Framework:

- **Professionalism**
  Identify and behave as a professional social worker committed to professional development.

- **Values and ethics**
  Apply social work ethical principles and values to guide professional practice.

- **Diversity**
  Recognise diversity and apply anti-discriminatory and anti-oppressive principles in practice.

- **Critical reflection and analysis**
  Apply critical reflection and analysis to inform and provide a rationale for professional decision-making.

- **Contexts and organisations**
  Engage with, inform, and adapt to changing contexts that shape practice. Operate effectively within your own organisational frameworks and contribute to the development of services and organisations. Operate effectively within multi-agency and inter-professional settings.

- **Professional leadership**
  Take responsibility for the professional learning and development of others through supervision, mentoring, assessing, research, teaching, leadership and management.

It will also introduce you to the following standards as set out in the 2008 social work subject benchmark statement.

- 5.5.2 **Gathering information.**
- 5.5.3 **Analysis and synthesis.**
- 5.6 **Communication skills.**
- 5.7 **Skills in working with others.**

This chapter is a narrative account from the perspective of a newly qualified social worker. It is important to make the reader aware that this is a reflection on one experience to aid social work learning. All the content is from one point of view; therefore please appreciate that it does not claim to be fact or research. The chapter is an honest and truthful account of the experiences and opinions of one individual. It is aimed at social work students who want to gain an insight into how personalisation ideologies and practice has impacted on one social work student.

A little about me

I am a newly qualified social worker with one year's post-qualifying experience working in the voluntary sector. I currently work for a not-for-profit organisation that focuses on social inclusion and enhancing an individual's well-being by providing meaningful activities and person-centred support. This way of working is heavily based on social model principles and a personalisation value base. The organisation is accessed by adults who experience psychological and/or emotional distress. As part of my varied role I provide support to individuals accessing the service, I co-ordinate a team of volunteers, supervise the social work students on placement and I also support various personalisation projects that the organisation has developed and drives forward.

When I was first asked to contribute towards this book I was thrilled and incredibly honoured. However, these feelings soon transformed into sheer panic and worry as I thought, I'm not a social work lecturer, nor am I an experienced social worker, nor do I claim to be an expert in personalisation. During my state of panic I sent several emails to Ali checking that she had asked the right person to do the job; her response was *I just want your passion and intelligence.* So I came to my own conclusion: through the use of narrative I will openly share my experiences of social work, personalisation and my passion for both. However, I can only attempt to demonstrate my intelligence; I will allow the reader to be the judge of that.

Why use narrative?

Throughout this chapter I put myself in the story-teller position, providing you with an insight into my life. I feel that it is important for you to you know about my life experiences to understand why I'm so passionate about personalisation today. Narrative is a powerful tool and by applying it to myself I have found writing this chapter to be an extremely challenging but therapeutic process. It has proved to be an effective tool as it has involved finding out what is important to me. Ali said in the first edition of this book, *the individual understands his or her own world according to his or her past experiences* (Gardner, 2011, p. 81).

Narrative is a form of story-telling that enables social workers to focus on the meaning of what the person is saying and discover what truly matters to them. By using this method we are able to understand individuals in a more personalised and meaningful way. Goodley (2001) believes that the use of narrative allows us to explore lived experiences and preserve a sense of the individual.

In my opinion, the use of narrative should automatically be used by all social workers when supporting individuals. However, due to structures, pressures and deadlines that are enforced upon us, this way of working can often be lost. Social workers are often left with no option but to quickly focus on sorting an individual's problems, providing a responsive service rather than listening to the person's problems and supporting them to find their own solution.

Why did I study social work?

My first *real* job was when I worked as a support worker supporting children and young individuals with visual impairments and learning disabilities in various different settings such as residential and 'special' schools/colleges. I thoroughly enjoyed this work as I built strong relationships with the individuals who accessed the services and supported them to learn independence skills. During my time as a support worker, I had a significant grievance with a social worker who made a disempowering decision for an individual I was key worker for. I was made to feel that my opinion on the decision was inferior and not valued (I can't imagine how the actual individual and family felt). Therefore, after much deliberation and to most people's surprise, I decided to study social work. This was obviously to further my career in the social care field but most importantly it was to discover for myself why social workers had so much power and could make decisions that could change people's lives for ever.

University

In my final year at university, I undertook the personalisation elective. The module was taught by an inspirational and passionate lecturer who made me feel motivated after every lecture. We focused on studying disability and looked at the very beginnings of social work from the charitable actions of churches in the 1900s, to the institutionalisation of disabled people, right through to the welfare state, the Disabled People's Movement and then focusing on the Right to Control in the present day. This detailed historical context really painted the picture for me and enabled me to understand why the personalisation agenda is so important for many oppressed social groups. It also made me question my own values, such as shifting them from the *helping* to *supporting* perspective.

It is important to state here that values are an essential tool that social workers should use to understand the decisions they make and the views they have. Adams and Sheard (2013) state that *your values shape the person that you are today and it is a key requirement of all social workers to understand their values* (p. 27). I've found that my values have changed profoundly since being a support worker compared to what they are now being a qualified social worker.

During the personalisation module I learnt how real social work should be and how oppressive the current social care system actually is. My own values were affected by guest speakers who came in and shared their personal experiences of how the personalisation agenda had impacted upon them: for example, through receiving personal budgets that gave them the choice to choose what services they received. This was a whole new concept to me.

Through the teaching I found that personalisation places the individual in the driving seat of their own care, support and needs, which empowers the person to make decisions about their lives. It moves away from the negative label of *service user*, indicating that a person is dependent upon services. Personalisation favours seeing the person as an *individual* who has strengths and who can be supported to live their life rather than merely existing. Ultimately, this emphasises that the individual is the expert of his or her own life.

Personalisation is a way of thinking and doing that turns traditional social work on its head; social workers no longer act as the professional who dictates to the service user. Personalisation highlights that social workers should be working in partnership and supporting the individual to live their life how they wish. These empowering values were what I was searching for; it was the one thing on the whole course that clearly made sense to me, and I remember thinking that this was the reason why I wanted to be a social worker. I felt that the personalisation module was the reason I came to university; it provided me with the fire in my belly that I needed to go out into the real world and support people to live rather than just exist. However, I soon found the experience of going out on placement with this radical new way of thinking was not going to be easy.

After the personalisation module finished I started my final placement with an organisation that provides supported living to older adults with learning disabilities in the community. When I started the placement, I was motivated and inspired, fresh from finishing the personalisation elective, naively thinking I could empower everyone. However, on the first day I witnessed bad practice, which immediately left me feeling deflated. As time went on I felt that the fire in my belly was slowly dying out.

On the whole, I found that the staff I was working with in this particular team were not interested in supporting the individuals in a creative or meaningful way. They just saw their support as a job: for example, go to work, dress the person, feed them, give them some money, take them to the shops, bath them, then clock off. It seemed that it was not part of their job description to actually communicate with the individual to ask them what they wanted and acknowledge them as human beings. When I tried to question this approach, I felt that I was speaking in a different language, plus I felt powerless in my student role.

After this, I witnessed how personalisation can be abused when I observed an annual review assessment. One of the individuals I was supporting on placement had their social worker visit the house to carry out a review of their care. The social worker went straight to the office, questioned the staff about risk assessments, finances and health action plans that were all part of the care plan. The remainder of the assessment involved checking paperwork and asking the staff questions. Eventually the individual (who the assessment was for) knocked on the office door and asked to come in. At this stage, I was already horrified that the individual was not included in their own assessment.

The individual came in and the social worker said, 'So, do you still like living here?' The individual said, 'Yeah', and that was the main interaction during the visit. When the social worker packed up their belongings they said, 'Oh yeah, I forgot to ask, have you heard about this personalisation thing and the Right to Control?' I spoke up and said that I knew about it. However, to my disbelief the social worker turned around and said:

'Oh well, not to worry, it doesn't really apply to them because they have lived here for such a long time and are happy. It will probably just cause aggravation so they don't need to be told about it.' This shocked and horrified me, especially after everything I had learnt. I remember thinking, why is personalisation so much more complex in practice and why don't social workers know about it? I did consider that the social worker probably had a limited understanding and wasn't confident in explaining the Right to Control, but I found this to be very disheartening and oppressive for the individual.

Afterwards I spent a great amount of time reflecting on this experience and it made me realise that the 'rosy picture' of personalisation I had learnt was perhaps an unrealistic concept in reality. Despite my negative experience, I still felt determined to be part of the new wave of social workers going out into practice spreading the positive personalisation message. I felt and still do feel devoted to the message and what it stands for, that being: everyone should be able to exercise choice in what they do with their lives, it just makes sense!

Where am I today and what are the challenges?

As described earlier, I presently have several roles including that of supervising the social work students on placement with us. I thoroughly enjoy this part of my job because as a professional I am constantly learning from the students. I strongly feel that it is important to promote personalisation principles in all aspects of my practice, including supervising the students. I try to do this by recognising that each student comes to the organisation with their own strengths and skills that they can draw upon and use while with us. I also try to actively encourage the students to explore personal budgets with the individuals they are supporting.

However, the students' limited understanding around personal budgets and personalisation has proved to be a challenge. The personalisation agenda and social model values are not subjects I can easily teach, nor should it be my place to. I was lucky enough to learn about them because I chose to take the personalisation elective on offer at university. Ultimately I feel that this highlights a crucial point – that students must be equipped with knowledge around the roots of personalisation, which stem from disability studies, before they start their placements.

In my opinion, the values of the social model of disability, the values of personalisation and the values of social work go hand in hand; you cannot learn one without the other. So it terrifies me that the module isn't even a mandatory part of the degree. Harris and Roulstone (2010) claim that *there are strong messages emerging that the on-going implementation of the personalisation agenda will only be effective if it is grounded in the work of the disabled people's movement and disability studies* (cited in Morgan, 2012, p. 216).

For personalisation to truly work we also need to educate and inform all new and practising social workers who have not been taught personalisation principles. A straightforward way of starting this process is ensuring that personalisation is embedded within the social work curriculum. By doing this it will hopefully influence the way new social workers perceive service users and the role they play in providing services. I realise that nothing is going to change overnight but if we can start to spread the personalisation way of thinking then it will eventually start to have an impact.

Using your social work degree in different ways

As well as making the personalisation module mandatory on the social work degree, I feel that teaching around the *social enterprise* model should also be included in this change. A clear definition of social enterprise is *a business that trades for a social and/or environmental purpose. It will have a clear sense of its 'social mission': which means it will know what difference it is trying to make, who it aims to help, and how it plans to do it* (Social Enterprise UK, 2013).

I have to be honest and state that I do not have a vast knowledge of social enterprises; the little understanding I do have has been acquired through working in the voluntary sector that is increasingly becoming dominated by this model of delivery. But what I do know about social enterprises is that they are positive, they move away from the current paternalistic culture of social work, and they promote the importance of community support. In relation to this, the charity In Control has set out a 2020 vision for personalisation whereby we strive for *a better tomorrow and a freer, fairer society with people at its heart, if people fall ill, become lonely, confused or are disabled, they are still valued and their community supports them* (In Control, 2010).

I think it will be extremely useful for students to have an understanding of social enterprises especially in the current climate where jobs are limited. There is a diverse range of employment opportunities in which social workers can employ their skills and knowledge. It is important that social work educators, in partnership with employers, support students to explore the range of options available in all sectors of social care. In 2011, research highlighted that *almost two-thirds of the British public would prefer their local services to be delivered by social enterprises* (Mills, 2011).

Ultimately, I am a firm believer that you can and should use your social work degree/qualification in different creative ways. I would argue that as social workers we are equipped to be forward-thinking and radical professionals pushing boundaries and setting up social enterprises to meet people's needs, rather than slotting them into existing services. The voluntary sector needs to maintain and attract qualified social workers. The values, skills and knowledge upon which social work is based are key ingredients in supporting individuals to exercise choice and control in their own lives.

My final thoughts

I am constantly left thinking, what does social work mean to me? At the moment, if I am totally honest, I feel like the odd one out because I don't work in a children's or statutory service. I feel pressured to work in a job where I should expect an income of around £22,000 to £28,000 and if I don't then it is easy for people to question if I am a real social worker. I feel that the true meaning of social work has become lost but the ideas and values embedded in personalisation are providing a glimpse of hope of getting that true meaning back. I now call my niche 'personalisation' and in the future I would love to set up a social enterprise with like-minded professionals that supports individuals to choose what support and services they want. To my current and future colleagues, peers and social work students I might seem naive, but I will hold on to my vision no matter what.

CHAPTER SUMMARY

The personalisation module has considerably impacted upon my views and values and has empowered me as a professional. Learning about personalisation touched a nerve with me and sparked my passion because it 'just made sense'. I will take what I have learnt and use it in all future practice when supporting individuals and supervising future social work students. I will also use it to ensure that I am involved in new initiatives such as setting up social enterprises and meeting needs in a more creative and community focused way. Furthermore, I hope one day if I am ever in the position where I need services or support, I will have the freedom and choice to choose what I want instead of someone else doing it for me.

ACTIVITY 8.1

In this chapter I have highlighted the importance of values in practice. Can you reflect on your work or practice placement experiences and identify examples where individuals have been denied choices? How could you use your understanding of personalisation to address a similar situation in future? How might you manage this with a staff group who were less informed and/or motivated by the principles and practice of personalisation?

COMMENT

The ability to put your values into practice can be challenging. As a student you can experience feelings of isolation and powerlessness in organisations. It is a good idea to reflect on the reasons for this lack of appetite for personalisation. Is it due to a lack of knowledge or training or perhaps due to a fear of working in a different way or even a threat to the current social work role? It is important that you acknowledge the reason why staff might be finding it hard to engage with the concept, so that you can work positively to effect change. Finally, it is useful to identify and engage with individuals and networks who can support you to inject enthusiasm to those who are less knowledge-able or motivated by the principles of personalisation. There are several organisations that are mentioned throughout this book. In addition social media such as Twitter offers an excellent opportunity to keep up to date and share your thinking with others. Some of the leading tweeters currently include:

Ermintude @Ermintude2
Gill Phillips @WhoseShoes
Martin Routledge @mroutled
Sarah Carr @SchrebersSister

Conclusion

At the time of writing this second edition, personalisation as a concept has emerged as a central feature in government policy relating to the public sector and in particular social care. The Coalition government clearly views personalisation as central to the delivery of social care support in the twenty-first century, drawing parallels with their vision of a *Big Society* and notions of *choice, control and consumerism*. An appetite for personalisation continues to grow but so too does ambivalence by many who are suspicious of the current enthusiasm expressed by a government responsible for reducing social care budgets and raising thresholds of eligibility. The political context of personalisation has been developed as a common thread throughout the book, recognising and analysing the way in which concepts of welfare have emerged and developed. The text has highlighted the significance of service user voice and its powerful influence in the development of self-directed support.

It is hoped that the reader has begun to understand the legislative, policy and practice models that have been developed for different service user groups and their carers in relation to self-directed support. The book has explored the subtle, yet significant, differences between care management and self-directed support using service user narrative to demonstrate some of the key themes and outcomes of this way of working. In addition, the inclusion of narrative has challenged the reader to consider broader issues of discrimination and empowerment that underpin one's understanding of personalisation.

Principally, personalisation is based on the person controlling and directing the support in a way that they believe will meet their needs. The book has considered how one of the key tensions surrounding choice and risk can be addressed within this framework. Drawing on research, practice experience and student activities, the book has attempted to provide a balanced picture of these contentious issues. Mindful of the polarisation of this debate, the book has considered some of the possible consequences for the social work role in the future.

While the book encourages students to adopt an evidence-based approach to their practice, it also recognises that many questions and uncertainties remain in relation to the implementation of personalisation. The future of adult social care is set to change dramatically and there are huge question marks in relation to the shape and function of the social work role. Qualifying students need to recognise the challenging contexts within which they will work. They also need to consider how they will adopt a questioning approach towards the way structures, organisations and practitioners adapt and respond to changing agendas, tasks and roles.

Fundamentally, the book has attempted to reinforce the need to bring together social work values and emerging practice by encouraging the reader to develop a radical engagement with key concepts and practical, effective solutions. In this way it provides an opportunity to embrace personalisation as more than a repackaged way of working but rather as a new paradigm of good practice.

Appendix 1

Professional Capabilities Framework

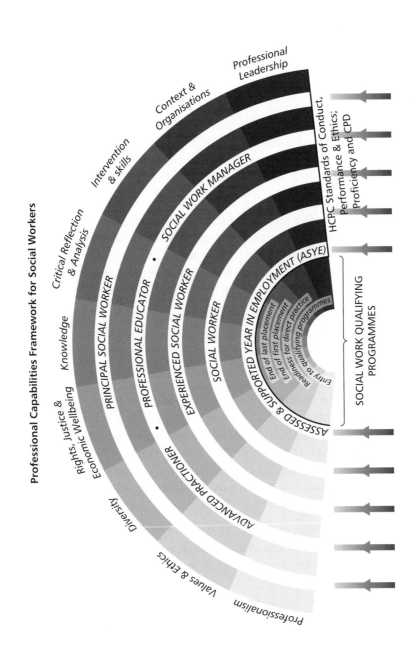

Appendix 2
Subject benchmark for social work

4 Defining principles

4.1 As an applied academic subject, social work is characterised by a distinctive focus on practice in complex social situations to promote and protect individual and collective well-being. This underscores the importance of partnerships between HEIs and service providers to ensure the full involvement of practitioners, managers, tutors, service users and carers with students in both academic and practice learning and assessment.

4.2 At honours level, the study of social work involves the integrated study of subject-specific knowledge, skills and values and the critical application of research knowledge from the social and human sciences, and from social work (and closely related domains) to inform understanding and to underpin action, reflection and evaluation. Honours degree programmes should be designed to help foster this integration of contextual, analytic, critical, explanatory and practical understanding.

4.3 Contemporary definitions of social work as a degree subject reflect its origins in a range of different academic and practice traditions. The precise nature and scope of the subject is itself a matter for legitimate study and critical debate. Three main issues are relevant to this.

- Social work is located within different social welfare contexts. Within the UK there are different traditions of social welfare (influenced by legislation, historical development and social attitudes) and these have shaped both social work education and practice in community-based settings including residential, day care and substitute care. In an international context, distinctive national approaches to social welfare policy, provision and practice have greatly influenced the focus and content of social work degree programmes.

- There are competing views in society at large on the nature of social work and on its place and purpose. Social work practice and education inevitably reflect these differing perspectives on the role of social work in relation to social justice, social care and social order.

- Social work, both as occupational practice and as an academic subject, evolves, adapts and changes in response to the social, political and economic challenges and demands of contemporary social welfare policy, practice and legislation.

4.4 Honours graduates in social work should therefore be equipped both to understand, and to work within, this context of contested debate about nature, scope and purpose, and be enabled to analyse, adapt to, manage and eventually to lead the processes of change.

4.5 The applied nature of social work as an academic subject means that practice is an essential and core element of learning. The following points clarify the use of the term 'practice' in the statement.

- The term 'practice' in this statement is used to encompass learning that takes place not only in professional practice placements, but also in a variety of other experiential learning situations. All learning opportunities that bear academic credit must be subject to methods of assessment appropriate to their academic level and be assessed by competent assessors. Where they form part of the curriculum leading to integrated academic and professional awards, practice learning opportunities will also be subject to regulations that further define learning requirements, standards and modes of assessment.

- In honours degree programmes covered by this statement, practice as an activity refers to experiential, action-based learning. In this sense, practice provides opportunities for students to improve and demonstrate their understanding and competence through the application and testing of knowledge and skills.

- Practice activity is also a source of transferable learning in its own right. Such learning can transfer both from a practice setting to the 'classroom' and vice versa. Thus practice can be as much a source of intellectual and cognitive learning as other modes of study. For this reason, learning through practice attracts full academic credit.

- Learning in practice can include activities such as observation, shadowing, analysis and research, as well as intervention within social work and related organisations. Practice-learning on honours degrees involves active engagement with service users and others in practice settings outside the university, and may involve, for example, virtual/simulated practice, observational and research activities.

4.6 Social work is a moral activity that requires practitioners to recognise the dignity of the individual, but also to make and implement difficult decisions (including restriction of liberty) in human situations that involve the potential for benefit or harm. Honours degree programmes in social work therefore involve the study, application of, and critical reflection upon, ethical principles and dilemmas. As reflected by the four care councils' codes of practice, this involves showing respect for persons, honouring the diverse and distinctive organisations and communities that make up contemporary society, promoting social justice and combating processes that lead to discrimination, marginalisation and social exclusion. This means that honours undergraduates must learn to:

- recognise and work with the powerful links between intrapersonal and interpersonal factors and the wider social, legal, economic, political and cultural context of people's lives;

- understand the impact of injustice, social inequalities and oppressive social relations;

- challenge constructively individual, institutional and structural discrimination;

- practise in ways that maximise safety and effectiveness in situations of uncertainty and incomplete information

- help people to gain, regain or maintain control of their own affairs, insofar as this is compatible with their own or others' safety, well-being and rights;

- work in partnership with service users and carers and other professionals to foster dignity, choice and independence, and effect change.

4.7 The expectation that social workers will be able to act effectively in such complex circumstances requires that honours degree programmes in social work should be designed to help students learn to become accountable, reflective, critical and evaluative. This involves learning to:

- think critically about the complex social, legal, economic, political and cultural contexts in which social work practice is located;

- work in a transparent and responsible way, balancing autonomy with complex, multiple and sometimes contradictory accountabilities (for example, to different service users, employing agencies, professional bodies and the wider society);

- exercise authority within complex frameworks of accountability and ethical and legal boundaries;

- acquire and apply the habits of critical reflection, self-evaluation and consultation, and make appropriate use of research in decision-making about practice and in the evaluation of outcomes.

5 Subject knowledge, understanding and skills
Subject knowledge and understanding

5.1 During their degree studies in social work, honours graduates should acquire, critically evaluate, apply and integrate knowledge and understanding in the following five core areas of study.

5.1.1 Social work services, service users and carers, which include:

- the social processes (associated with, for example, poverty, migration, unemployment, poor health, disablement, lack of education and other sources of disadvantage) that lead to marginalisation, isolation and exclusion, and their impact on the demand for social work services;

- explanations of the links between definitional processes contributing to social differences (for example, social class, gender, ethnic differences, age, sexuality and religious belief) to the problems of inequality and differential need faced by service users;

- the nature of social work services in a diverse society (with particular reference to concepts such as prejudice, interpersonal, institutional and structural discrimination, empowerment and anti-discriminatory practices);

- the nature and validity of different definitions of, and explanations for, the characteristics and circumstances of service users and the services required by them, drawing on knowledge from research, practice experience, and from service users and carers;

- the focus on outcomes, such as promoting the well-being of young people and their families, and promoting dignity, choice and independence for adults receiving services;

- the relationship between agency policies, legal requirements and professional boundaries in shaping the nature of services provided in interdisciplinary contexts and the issues associated with working across professional boundaries and within different disciplinary groups.

5.1.2 *The service delivery context, which includes:*

- the location of contemporary social work within historical, comparative and global perspectives, including European and international contexts;

- the changing demography and cultures of communities in which social workers will be practising;

- the complex relationships between public, social and political philosophies, policies and priorities and the organisation and practice of social work, including the contested nature of these;

- the issues and trends in modern public and social policy and their relationship to contemporary practice and service delivery in social work;

- the significance of legislative and legal frameworks and service delivery standards (including the nature of legal authority, the application of legislation in practice, statutory accountability and tensions between statute, policy and practice);

- the current range and appropriateness of statutory, voluntary and private agencies providing community-based, day-care, residential and other services and the organisational systems inherent within these;

- the significance of inter-relationships with other related services, including housing, health, income maintenance and criminal justice (where not an integral social service);

- the contribution of different approaches to management, leadership and quality in public and independent human services;

- the development of personalised services, individual budgets and direct payments;

- the implications of modern information and communications technology (ICT) for both the provision and receipt of services.

5.1.3 Values and ethics, which include:

- the nature, historical evolution and application of social work values;

- the moral concepts of rights, responsibility, freedom, authority and power inherent in the practice of social workers as moral and statutory agents;

- the complex relationships between justice, care and control in social welfare and the practical and ethical implications of these, including roles as statutory agents and in upholding the law in respect of discrimination;

- aspects of philosophical ethics relevant to the understanding and resolution of value dilemmas and conflicts in both interpersonal and professional contexts;

- the conceptual links between codes defining ethical practice, the regulation of professional conduct and the management of potential conflicts generated by the codes held by different professional groups.

5.1.4 Social work theory, which includes:

- research-based concepts and critical explanations from social work theory and other disciplines that contribute to the knowledge base of social work, including their distinctive epistemological status and application to practice;

- the relevance of sociological perspectives to understanding societal and structural influences on human behaviour at individual, group and community levels;

- the relevance of psychological, physical and physiological perspectives to understanding personal and social development and functioning;

- social science theories explaining group and organisational behaviour, adaptation and change;

- models and methods of assessment, including factors underpinning the selection and testing of relevant information, the nature of professional judgement and the processes of risk assessment and decision-making

- approaches and methods of intervention in a range of settings, including factors guiding the choice and evaluation of these;

- user-led perspectives;

- knowledge and critical appraisal of relevant social research and evaluation methodologies, and the evidence base for social work.

5.1.5 The nature of social work practice, which includes:

- the characteristics of practice in a range of community-based and organisational settings within statutory, voluntary and private sectors, and the factors influencing changes and developments in practice within these contexts;

- the nature and characteristics of skills associated with effective practice, both direct and indirect, with a range of service users and in a variety of settings;

- the processes that facilitate and support service user choice and independence;

- the factors and processes that facilitate effective interdisciplinary, inter-professional and inter-agency collaboration and partnership;

- the place of theoretical perspectives and evidence from international research in assessment and decision-making processes in social work practice;

- the integration of theoretical perspectives and evidence from international research into the design and implementation of effective social work intervention, with a wide range of service users, carers and others;

- the processes of reflection and evaluation, including familiarity with the range of approaches for evaluating service and welfare outcomes, and their significance for the development of practice and the practitioner.

Subject-specific skills and other skills

5.2 As an applied subject at honours degree level, social work necessarily involves the development of skills that may be of value in many situations (for example, analytical thinking, building relationships, working as a member of an organisation, intervention, evaluation and reflection). Some of these skills are specific to social work but many are also widely transferable. What helps to define the specific nature of these skills in a social work context are:

- the context in which they are applied and assessed (e.g. communication skills in practice with people with sensory impairments or assessment skills in an interprofessional setting);

- the relative weighting given to such skills within social work practice (e.g. the central importance of problem-solving skills within complex human situations);

- the specific purpose of skill development (e.g the acquisition of research skills in order to build a repertoire of research-based practice);

- a requirement to integrate a range of skills (i.e. not simply to demonstrate these in an isolated and incremental manner).

5.3 All social work honours graduates should show the ability to reflect on and learn from the exercise of their skills. They should understand the significance of the concepts of continuing professional development and lifelong learning, and accept responsibility for their own continuing development.

5.4 Social work honours graduates should acquire and integrate skills in the following five core areas.

Problem-solving skills

5.5 These are subdivided into four areas.

5.5.1 Managing problem-solving activities:
honours graduates in social work should be able to plan problem-solving activities, i.e. to:

- think logically, systematically, critically and reflectively;
- apply ethical principles and practices critically in planning problem-solving activities;
- plan a sequence of actions to achieve specified objectives, making use of research, theory and other forms of evidence;
- manage processes of change, drawing on research, theory and other forms of evidence.

5.5.2 Gathering information:
honours graduates in social work should be able to:

- gather information from a wide range of sources and by a variety of methods, for a range of purposes. These methods should include electronic searches, reviews of relevant literature, policy and procedures, face-to-face interviews, written and telephone contact with individuals and groups;
- take into account differences of viewpoint in gathering information and critically assess the reliability and relevance of the information gathered;
- assimilate and disseminate relevant information in reports and case records.

5.5.3 Analysis and synthesis:
honours graduates in social work should be able to analyse and synthesise knowledge gathered for problem-solving purposes, i.e. to:

- assess human situations, taking into account a variety of factors (including the views of participants, theoretical concepts, research evidence, legislation and organisational policies and procedures);
- analyse information gathered, weighing competing evidence and modifying their viewpoint in light of new information, then relate this information to a particular task, situation or problem;
- consider specific factors relevant to social work practice (such as risk, rights, cultural differences and linguistic sensitivities, responsibilities to protect vulnerable individuals and legal obligations);
- assess the merits of contrasting theories, explanations, research, policies and procedures;
- synthesise knowledge and sustain reasoned argument;

- employ a critical understanding of human agency at the macro (societal), mezzo (organisational and community) and micro (inter and intrapersonal) levels;

- critically analyse and take account of the impact of inequality and discrimination in work with people in particular contexts and problem situations.

5.5.4 *Intervention and evaluation:*

honours graduates in social work should be able to use their knowledge of a range of interventions and evaluation processes selectively to:

- build and sustain purposeful relationships with people and organisations in community-based, and inter-professional contexts;

- make decisions, set goals and construct specific plans to achieve these, taking into account relevant factors including ethical guidelines;

- negotiate goals and plans with others, analysing and addressing in a creative manner human, organisational and structural impediments to change;

- implement plans through a variety of systematic processes that include working in partnership;

- undertake practice in a manner that promotes the well-being and protects the safety of all parties;

- engage effectively in conflict resolution;

- support service users to take decisions and access services, with the social worker as navigator, advocate and supporter;

- manage the complex dynamics of dependency and, in some settings, provide direct care and personal support in everyday living situations;

- meet deadlines and comply with external definitions of a task;

- plan, implement and critically review processes and outcomes;

- bring work to an effective conclusion, taking into account the implications for all involved;

- monitor situations, review processes and evaluate outcomes;

- use and evaluate methods of intervention critically and reflectively.

Communication skills

5.6 Honours graduates in social work should be able to communicate clearly, accurately and precisely (in an appropriate medium) with individuals and groups in a range of formal and informal situations, i.e. to:

- make effective contact with individuals and organisations for a range of objectives, by verbal, paper-based and electronic means;

- clarify and negotiate the purpose of such contacts and the boundaries of their involvement;

- listen actively to others, engage appropriately with the life experiences of service users, understand accurately their viewpoint and overcome personal prejudices to respond appropriately to a range of complex personal and interpersonal situations;

- use both verbal and non-verbal cues to guide interpretation;

- identify and use opportunities for purposeful and supportive communication with service users within their everyday living situations;

- follow and develop an argument and evaluate the viewpoints of, and evidence presented by, others;

- write accurately and clearly in styles adapted to the audience, purpose and context of the communication;

- use advocacy skills to promote others' rights, interests and needs;

- present conclusions verbally and on paper, in a structured form, appropriate to the audience for which these have been prepared;

- make effective preparation for, and lead meetings in a productive way;

- communicate effectively across potential barriers resulting from differences (for example, in culture, language and age).

Skills in working with others

5.7 Honours graduates in social work should be able to work effectively with others, i.e. to:

- involve users of social work services in ways that increase their resources, capacity and power to influence factors affecting their lives;

- consult actively with others, including service users and carers, who hold relevant information or expertise;

- act co-operatively with others, liaising and negotiating across differences such as organisational and professional boundaries and differences of identity or language;

- develop effective helping relationships and partnerships with other individuals, groups and organisations that facilitate change;

- act with others to increase social justice by identifying and responding to prejudice, institutional discrimination and structural inequality;

- act within a framework of multiple accountability (for example, to agencies, the public, service users, carers and others);

- challenge others when necessary, in ways that are most likely to produce positive outcomes.

Skills in personal and professional development

5.8 Honours graduates in social work should be able to:

- advance their own learning and understanding with a degree of independence;
- reflect on and modify their behaviour in the light of experience;
- identify and keep under review their own personal and professional boundaries;
- manage uncertainty, change and stress in work situations;
- handle inter and intrapersonal conflict constructively;
- understand and manage changing situations and respond in a flexible manner;
- challenge unacceptable practices in a responsible manner;
- take responsibility for their own further and continuing acquisition and use of knowledge and skills;
- use research critically and effectively to sustain and develop their practice.

Glossary

Co-production   This is a term used to describe a process whereby service users and the wider community are involved in designing services, support and solutions. The premise of co-production is that those using services are best placed to advise and design support. This process requires power being shared with service users to empower them to identify solutions. Co-production spans both local services/support to building social capital.

Direct payment   This is a cash payment given to service users in lieu of services. The important issue in relation to personalisation is that direct payments legislation has made it permissible for local authorities to give service users money. Basically it is the mechanism required for transferring the money from the local authority to the service user.

Independent living movement   This represents a worldwide movement of disabled people who proclaim to work for self-determinism, self-respect and equal opportunities. The movement emerged in the early 1970s with the development of Independent Centres for Independence. Advocates promote a way of looking at disability and society which promotes the social model of disability and believes that preconceived notions and a predominantly medical view of disability contribute to negative attitudes towards disabled people.

Independent living   This is one of the goals of personalisation. It does not necessarily mean living on your own or doing things alone but focuses on people having a choice and control over the assistance and or equipment needed to go about their daily life.

Indicative budget/indicative allocation   Once an assessment is complete, the local authority will use the resource allocation system to identify the level of financial support required. The service user is then informed of this amount of money. This knowledge helps the service user develop a support plan. Once the support plan has been agreed, the indicative budget will then become an actual budget and is given to the service user. It is called an indicative budget as the money cannot be transferred to the individual until the local authority is satisfied that the support plan will meet the needs identified in the assessment.

Individual budget   Individual budgets include the money from the local authority as described under **Personal budget**, but it also involves bringing together different funding streams besides social care. This might include all or some of the following: local authority adult social care; integrated community equipment services; Disabled Facilities Grants; Supporting People for housing-related support; Access to Work and Independent Living Fund. This money is pooled to allow the service user flexibility in meeting their needs. Service users may choose to receive it as cash or services or a mixture of both. The terms 'personal budget' and 'individual budget' are starting to be used interchangeably by some local authorities. This has caused confusion for service users and social workers alike but the notions of choice, control and flexibility underpin both definitions.

Outcome-focused review   The support plan will identify a number of outcomes that the service user wants to achieve and how support will be arranged to achieve these. The purpose of an outcome-focused review is to review progress in using the budget to achieve the outcomes set out in the support plan. During the review the support plan may also be updated and the council will check if the person is still eligible for social care.

Personal budget   This is the allocation of funding given to service users after an assessment. The service user can choose to take this money as a direct payment or can leave it with the local authority to commission the service or support. Either way it is important that the service user can choose how the money is spent. Importantly, service users know how much money has been allocated.
See also **Individual budget**.

Personalisation   This is the umbrella term used to encapsulate the government's agenda for the transformation of adult social care. The government use this term broadly to refer to individuals having as much choice and control in the way support is designed and delivered as possible and ensuring that universal and community support and services are available and accessible to everyone.

Person-centred planning   This focuses on supporting individuals to live as independently as possible, having choice and control wherever possible. Person-centred planning places the individual at the centre of the process and builds support, networks and services around them.

Resource allocation system (RAS)   This is a system used by most local authorities to work out the financial resources which will be allocated to the individual and takes place after the assessment.

Self-assessment Service users are given the opportunity to assess their own needs. This usually involves completing a self-assessment questionnaire whereby the service user scores their needs against a set of domains.

Self-directed support   This idea forms the basis of personalisation. Service users are seen as the experts in their own lives. They are best placed to know what is best for them. No matter how service users choose to receive social care, the notion of self-determination should be fully embraced.

Support brokerage   This is a term used to describe a range of tasks and functions carried out by an individual or organisation to support a service user to design, arrange and manage their support.

Support planning   This is the process whereby service users can identify how they would like to live their life and choose the support or services that will help them make the changes. The support plan must identify how the budget will be spent, how it will meet the outcomes and how the person will stay in control of the plan.

Trust   A trust can be a group of people made up of family and friends, chosen by the person receiving the budget. Individuals can also choose to employ a private or voluntary organisation that can look after the individual's budget on their behalf. An individual will usually have to make a payment to the organisation for this support.

References

Action on Elder Abuse (2004) *Hidden voices: Older people's experience of abuse. An analysis of calls to the action on elder abuse helpline.* London: Help the Aged.

Adams, J and Sheard, A (2013) *Positive social work: The essential toolkit for NQSWs.* Critical Publishing.

Adams, R, Dominelli, L and Payne, M (2009) *Critical practice in social work.* Exeter: Palgrave Macmillan.

ADASS (2005) *Safeguarding adults: A national framework of standards for good practice in adult protection work.* London: ADASS.

ADASS (2009) *Common resource allocation framework.* London: ADASS.

ADASS (2013) *Social care funding: 'a bleak outlook is getting bleaker'.* London: ADASS. **www.adass.org.uk**.

Allen, J, Neill, M, Woodhead, N, Reid, S, Erwin, L and Sanderson, H (2008) *Person-centred risk course book.* Stockport: HSA Press.

Armstrong, D (2003) *Experiences of special education.* London: Routledge/Falmer.

Atkinson, D (2005) Narratives and people with learning disabilities, in Grant, G, Goward, P, Richardson, M and Ramcharan, P (eds) *Learning disability: A life cycle approach to valuing people.* Berkshire: Open University Press.

Atkinson, R (1998) *The life story interview. Qualitative research methods.* London: Sage.

Audit Commission (2010) *Financial management of personal budgets: Challenges and opportunities for councils.* London: Audit Commission.

Barnes, C and Mercer, G (2010) *Exploring disability* (2nd edn). Cambridge: Policy Press.

BASW (2002) *Code of ethics for social workers.* Birmingham: BASW.

BASW (2012) *The code of ethics for social workers: Statement of principles.* Birmingham: BASW.

Bates, P and Silberman, W (2007) *Modelling risk management in inclusive settings* (online). London: National Development Team.

Beresford, P (2003) *It's our lives: A short theory of knowledge, distance and experience.* London: Citizen Press.

Beresford, P and Andrews, E (2012) *Caring for our future: What service users say. Joseph Rowntree Foundation Programme Paper: Paying for long-term care.* Bristol: Brunel University Press and Shaping Our Lives.

Beresford, P and Hasler, F (2009) *Transforming social care: Changing the future together.* Bristol: Brunel University Press.

Bogg, D (2012) *Applying a personalised approach to eligibility criteria.* Maidenhead: Open University Press and Community Care.

Borsay, A (2005) *Disability and social policy in Britain since 1750: A history of exclusion.* Basingstoke: Palgrave Macmillan.

Boyle, D, Clark, S and Burns, S (2006) *Co-production by people outside paid employment.* York: Joseph Rowntree Foundation.

Braye, S and Preston-Shoot, M (2001) *Empowering practice in social care.* Buckingham: Open University Press.

Brookes, N, Callaghan, L, Netten, A and Fox, D (2013) Personalisation and innovation in a cold financial climate. *British Journal of Social Work* online, 5 June. doi:10.1093/bjsw/bct104.

Brown, H and Benson, S (1992) *A practical guide to working with people with learning disabilities: A handbook for care assistants and support workers.* London: Hawker Publications.

Buck, T and Smith, S (2003) *Poor relief or poor deal: The social fund, safety nets and social security.* Hampshire: Ashgate.

Burton, J, Toscano, T and Zonouzi, M (2012) *Personalisation for social workers: Opportunities and challenges for frontline practice.* Berkshire: Open University Press McGraw-Hill Education.

Carr, S (2011) Enabling risk and securing safety: Self-directed support and personal budgets. *Journal of Adult Protection*, 13 (3): 122–36.

Carr, S and Robbins, D (2009) *The implementation of individual budget schemes in adult social care. Research Briefing 20.* London: Social Care Institute for Excellence.

Children and Families Bill (2013) *Contextual information and responses to pre-legislative Scrutiny, February 2013.* **www.gov.uk**.

Chinn, C (1995) *Poverty amidst prosperity: The urban poor in England, 1834–1914.* Manchester: Manchester University Press.

Clark, H and Spafford, J (2001) Adapting to the culture of user control? *Social Work Education*, 21 (2): 247–57.

Clarke, J (2004) *Changing welfare, changing states: New directions in social policy.* London: Sage.

Community Care (2013) *State of personalisation survey 2013.* **www.communitycare.co.uk**.

Crosby, N, Kelly, G, Lazarus, C, Macintyre, L and Sibthorp, K (2012) *Building a new relationship with children, young people and families.* London: In Control. **www.in-control.org.uk**.

Davies, K (1998) The disabled people's movement – putting the power in empowerment. Paper for a seminar at Sheffield University. Sheffield: Sheffield University.

Department for Communities and Local Government (DCLG) (2008) *Rough sleeping strategy. No one left out: Communities ending rough sleeping.* London: DCLG.

Department for Education (2007) *Aiming high for disabled children.* London: Department for Education.

Department for Education (2011) *Support and aspiration: A new approach to special educational needs and disability. A consultation.* London: Department for Education.

Department for Education (2012) *Support and aspiration: A new approach to special educational needs and disability. Progress and next steps.* London: Department for Education.

Department for Work and Pensions (2005) *Opportunity age: Meeting the challenges of ageing in the 21st Century.* London: DWP.

Department of Health (1989) *Caring for people: Community care in the next decade and beyond.* London: HMSO.

Department of Health (1990) *The NHS and Community Care Act.* London: HMSO.

Department of Health (1991) *Care management and assessment: Summary of practice guidance.* London: Department of Health.

Department of Health (1998) *Modernising social services: Promoting independence, improving protection, raising standards.* London: Department of Health.

Department of Health (2000) *No secrets: Guidance on developing and implementing multi-agency policies and procedures to procedures to protect vulnerable adults from abuse.* London: Department of Health.

Department of Health (2001) *Valuing people: A new strategy for learning disability for the 21st century.* London: Department of Health.

Department of Health (2002) *Fair Access to Care Services: Guidance on Eligibility Criteria for Adult Social Care.* LAC (2002) 13. London: Department of Health.

Department of Health (2003a) *Fairer charging policies for home care and other non-residential social services: Guidance for councils with social services responsibilities.* London: Department of Health (revised 2013).

Department of Health (2003b) *Social services performance assessment framework indicators 2002–2003.* London: Department of Health.

Department of Health (2003c) *Fair access to care services – Guidance on eligibility for adult social care.* London: Department of Health.

Department of Health (2005) *Independence, well-being and choice: Our vision for the future of social care for adults in England.* London: Department of Health.

Department of Health (2006) *Our health, our care, our say: A new direction for community service.* London: Department of Health.

Department of Health (2007) *Independence, choice and risk: A guide to best practice in supported decision making. Annex A: A supported decision tool.* London: Department of Health.

Department of Health (2008a) *Putting people first: Working to make it happen. Adult social care workforce strategy – interim statement.* London: Department of Health.

Department of Health (2008b) *Good practice in support planning and brokerage: Putting people first personalisation toolkit.* London: Department of Health.

Department of Health (2009a) *Building a safe, confident future: The final report of the social work task force.* London: Department of Health.

Department of Health (2009b) *Report for consultation: The review of No secrets guidance.* London: Department of Health.

Department of Health (2010a) *Prioritising need in the context of putting people first: A whole system approach to eligibility for social care. Guidance on eligibility criteria for adult social care.* London: Department of Health.

Department of Health (2010b) *Fairer contributions guidance: Calculating an individual's contribution to their personal budget.* London: Department of Health.

Department of Health (2010c) *A vision for adult social care: Capable communities and active communities and active citizens.* London: Department of Health.

Department of Health (2012) *Caring for our future: reforming care and support.* London: Department of Health.

Department of Health (2013) *Integrated care and support: Our shared commitment.* London: Department of Health.

Department of Work and Pensions (2010) *Independent Living Fund. Written ministerial statement 13 December 2010.* London: Department of Work and Pensions. **www.dwp.gov.uk/docs/wms-ilf-131210. pdf.**

Dickie, E (2013) *A personalised approach to prison resettlement report.* London: Revolving Doors Agency. **www.revolving-doors.org.uk.**

Duffy, S (1996) *Unlocking the imagination: Purchasing services for people with learning difficulties.* London: Choice Press.

Duffy, S (2003) *Keys to citizenship: A guide to getting good support for people with learning disabilities.* Birkenhead: Paradigm.

Duffy, S (2004) In control. *Journal of Integrated Care,* 12 (6): 7–13.

Duffy, S (2006) *Keys to citizenship: A guide to getting good support for people with learning disabilities* (2nd edn). Birkenhead: Paradigm.

Duffy, S (2007) Care management and self-directed support. *Journal of Integrated Care,* 15 (5): 3–14.

Duffy, S (2009) *Self directed support: Social workers contribution paper.* Series paper. London: In Control.

Duffy, S (2010) *The future of personalisation: Implications for welfare reform.* Sheffield: Centre for Welfare Reform.

Duffy, S (2012) *Is personalisation dead?* London: Centre for Welfare Reform.

Dustin, D (2007) *The McDonaldization of social work.* Aldershot: Ashgate.

Edsall, C (1971) *The anti-poor law movement 1834–44.* Manchester: Manchester University Press.

Ellis, K (2007) Direct payments and social work practice: The significance of 'street-level bureaucracy in determining eligibility. *British Journal of Social Work,* 37: 405–22.

Englander, D (1998) *Poverty and the poor law reform in 19th century Britain 1834–1914: From Chadwick to Booth.* Essex: Longman.

Fennell, K (2011) Adult protection: The Scottish legislative framework, Chapter 4 in Scragg, T and Mantell, A (eds), *Safeguarding adults in social work* (2nd edn). Exeter: Learning Matters.

Ferguson, I (2007) Increasing user choice or privatizing risk? The antinomies of personalization. *British Journal of Social Work,* 37 (3): 387–403.

Finnegan, R H (1992) *Oral traditions and the verbal arts: A guide to research practices.* London: Routledge.

Flynn, M (2006) *Developing the role of personal assistants. Researched and compiled for a Skills for Care pilot project examining new and emerging roles in social care.* University of Sheffield, 28 March, LSE.

French, S and Swain, J (2006) Telling stories for a politics of hope. *Disability and Society,* 21 (5): 383–97.

Gardner, A (2011) *Personalisation in social work.* Exeter: Learning Matters.

Gilbert, T and Powell, J L (2011) Personalisation and sustainable care. *Journal of Care Services Management,* 5 (2): 27–30.

Glasby, J (2011) *Whose risk is it anyway? Risk and regulation in an era of personalisation.* York: Joseph Rowntree Foundation

Glasby, J and Littlechild, R (2009) *Direct payments and personal budgets: Putting personalisation into practice.* Bristol: Policy Press.

Glendinning, C, Challis, D, Fernandez, J-L, Jacobs, S, Jones, K, Knapp, M, Manthorpe, J, Moran, N, Netten, A, Stevens, M and Wilberforce, M (2008) *Evaluation of the individual budgets pilot programme. Final report.* University of York: Social Policy Research Unit.

Goodley, D (2001) Learning difficulties, the social model of disability and impairment: Challenging epistemologies. *Disability and Society*, 16: 207 –31.

Goodley, D, Lawthorn, R, Clough, P and Moore, M (2004) *Researching life stories: Theory and analyses in a biographical age.* London: Routledge Falmer.

Grant, G, Goward, P, Richardson, M and Ramcharan, R (eds) (2005) *Learning disability: A lifestyle approach to valuing people.* Buckingham: Open University Press.

Gray, A M and Birrell, D (2013) Personalisation in adult social care, Chapter 5 in *Transforming adult social care: contemporary policy and practice.* Bristol: Policy Press.

Guardian (2013) Health and social care 'join up' plans unveiled. 14 May.

Hatton, C, Waters, J and Routledge, M (2013) *National Personal Budgets Survey 2013: Summary of main fndings and next steps.* London: TLAP.

Hatton, C, Waters, J, Duffy, S, Senker, J, Crosby, N, Poll, C, Tyson, A, O'Brien, J and Towell, D (2008) *A report on In control's second phase: Evaluation and learning 2005–2007.* London: In Control.

HCPC (2012) *Standards of proficiency for social workers in England.* London: HCPC.

Henwood, M and Hudson, B (2007) *Here to stay? Self directed support: Aspiration and implementation. A review for the Department of Health.* Heathencote: Melanie Henwood Associates.

Henwood, M and Hudson, B (2008) *Lost to the system? The impact of fair access to care.* London: CSCI.

HM Government (2007) *Putting people first: A shared vision and commitment to the transformation of adult social care.* London: Home Office.

HM Government (2010) *The coalition: Our programme for government.* London: HM Government.

HM Government (2011) *Vision to end rough sleeping: No second night out nationwide.* London: Home Office.

Hough, J and Rice, B (2010) *Providing personalised support to rough sleepers: An evaluation of the City of London pilot.* York: Joseph Rowntree Foundation.

Hudson, B (1988) Doomed from the start? *Health Services Journal*, 23 June: 708 –9.

In Control (2007) *Making a support plan.* London: In Control.

In Control (2010) *Vision 2010: Real impact, real change.* Wythall: In Control.

Jay, D (1937) *The socialist case.* London: Faber and Faber.

Jones, S (2009) *Critical learning for social work students.* Exeter: Learning Matters.

Jones, S (2013) *Critical learning for social work students* (2nd edn). London: Sage/Learning Matters.

Jordan, B (1974) *Poor parents: Social policy and the 'cycle of deprivation'.* London: Routledge and Kegan Paul.

Kestenbaum, A (1993) *Making community care a reality: The independent living fund, 1988 – 1993.* London: RADAR.

Kinnaird, L (2010) *Let's get personal: Personalisation and dementia. A policy and research report.* Edinburgh: Alzheimer Scotland.

Kinsella, P (2000) *What are the barriers in relation to person centred planning?* York: Joseph Rowntree Foundation.

Land, H and Himmelweit, S (2010) *Who cares: who pays? A report on personalisation in social care.* London: Unison.

Leadbeater, C (2004*) Personalisation through participation: A new script for public services.* London: Demos.

Leece, J and Bornat, B (2006) *Developments in direct payments.* Bristol: Policy Press.

Leece, J and Leece, D (2011) Personalisation: Perceptions of the role of social work in a world of brokers and budgets. *British Journal of Social Work*, 4 (2): 204–23.

Lester, S (1999) From map-reader to map-maker: approaches to moving beyond knowledge and competence, Chapter 4 in O'Reilly, D, Cunningham, L and Lester, S (eds) *Developing the Capable Practitioner.* London: Kogan Page. Reproduced on the HE Academy website by kind permission of Taylor and Francis Ltd.

Lewis, J (1995) *The voluntary sector, the state and social work in Britain.* Aldershot: Edward Elgar.

Lightfoot, T (2010) *Dementia: Increasing awareness and uptake of direct payments and personal budgets.* London: Department of Health.

McDonald, A (2006) *Understanding community care: A guide for social workers* (2nd edn). Basingstoke: Palgrave Macmillan.

MacKay, D and MacIntyre, G (2011) Personalization and the role of the social worker, in Taylor, R, Hill, M and McNeill, F (eds) *Early professional development for social workers.* Birmingham: Venture Press.

McKenzie, P (2000) *A community response to abuse.* Abingdon: Routledge.

McNeill, F, Farrel, S, Lightowler, C and Maruna, S (2012) How and why people stop offending: Discovering desistance. **www.iriss.org.uk/resources/how-and-why-people-stop-offending-discovering-desistance**.

Manchester Evening News (2007) *NHS pays for season ticket.* 17 December.

Mandelstam, M (2013) *Safeguarding adults and the law* (2nd edn). London: Jessica Kingsley.

Marks, D (1999) Dimensions of oppression: Theorising the embodied subject. *Disability and Society*, 14: 611–26.

Marsh, P and Fisher, M (1992) *Good intentions: Developing partnership in social services.* York: Joseph Rowntree Foundation.

Marshall, J D (1985) *The old poor law 1795–1834* (2nd edn). London: Macmillan.

Marshall, T (1963) *Sociology at the crossroads.* London: Heinemann.

Marshall, T and Bottomore, T (1987) *Citizenship and social class.* London: Pluto Press.

Meyer, J and Land, R (2003) *Threshold Concepts and Troublesome Knowledge: Linkages to Ways of Thinking and Practicing within the Disciplines. Enhancing Teaching-Learning Environments in Undergraduate Courses Project Occasional Report 4.* **www.etl.tla.ed.ac.uk//docs/ETLreport4.pdf**.

Mills, M (2011) Where are Britain's 62,000 social enterprises? *The Guardian* online. **www.theguardian.com/social-enterprise-network/2011/nov/01/buyse-social-enterprise-directory**.

Mind (2013) *Personal health budgets in England: Making them work in mental health.* Mind: London. **www.cpft.nhs.uk**.

Ministry of Justice (2012) *Compendium of re-offending statistics and analysis.* **www.justice.gov.uk/statistics/reoffending/compendium-of-reoffending-statistics-and-analysis**.

Mitchell, W and Glendinning, C (2007) *A review of the research evidence surrounding risk perceptions, risk management strategies and their consequences in adult social care for different groups of service users.* Working Paper DHR 2180 01.07. York: Social Policy Research Unit, University of York.

Mitchell, W, Baxter, K and Glendinning, C (2012) *Updated review of research on risk and adult social care in England.* York: Joseph Rowntree Foundation.

Moore, D and Jones, K (2012) *Social work and dementia.* Exeter: Learning Matters.

Moore, D and Nicoll, T (2009) *Getting a blue life: Personalization and the criminal justice system.* London: Revolving Doors Agency. **www.revolving-doors.org.uk/search/?searchterm=Getting+a+Blue+Life&x=0&y=0**.

Morgan, H (2012) The social model of disability as a threshold concept: Troublesome knowledge and liminal spaces in social work education. *Social Work Education*, 31 (2): 215–26.

Morris, J (2004) *Social model assessment team pilot: Evaluation.* Essex Social Services.

Mullender, A and Ward, D (1991) *Self directed groupwork: Users take actions for empowerment.* London: Whiting and Birch.

National Audit Office (2011) *Oversight of users' choice and provider competition in care markets* (September). London: National Audit Office.

National Institute for Mental Health in England (2006) *Direct payments for people with mental health problems: A guide to action.* Care Services Improvement Partnership (CSIP). London: DH.

Needham, C and Carr, S (2009) *Co-production: An emerging evidence base for social care transformation.* London: SCIE.

NHS The Information Centre (2013) *Community care statistics: Social services activity – England, 2011–12, Final Release.* London: NHS.

ODI (Office for Disability Issues) (2009) *Government response to the consultation on the Right to Control.* London: ODI.

Oliver, M (1990) *The politics of disablement.* Basingstoke: Macmillan.

Oliver, M (2000) Why do insiders matter?, in Moore, M (ed.) *Insider perspectives on inclusion.* Sheffield: Phillip Armstrong.

Oliver, M and Sapey, B (1999) *Social work with disabled people* (2nd edn). Basingstoke: Macmillan.

Parker, J (2010) *Social work practice* (3rd edn). Exeter: Learning Matters.

Poll, C, Duffy, S, Hatton, C, Sanderson, H and Routledge, M (2006) *A report on In Control's first phase 2003–2005.* London: In Control.

Powell, M and Hewitt, M (2002) *Welfare state and welfare change.* Buckingham: Open University Press.

Priestley, M (2004) Tragedy strikes again! Why community care still poses a problem for integrated living, in Swain, J, French, S, Barnes, C and Thomas, C (eds) *Disabling barriers – Enabling environments.* London: Sage.

Prime Minister's Strategy Unit (2005) *Improving the life chances of disabled people.* London: Cabinet Office.

Pritchard, J (ed) (2009) *Good practice in the law and safeguarding adults.* London: Jessica Kingsley.

Pryor, S (2001) *The responsible prisoner.* **http://www.pfi.org/cot/prison/corrections/the-responsible-prisoner-uk/view**.

Quinney, A (2006) *Collaborative social work practice.* London: Learning Matters.

Renshaw, C (2008) Do self-assessment and self-directed support undermine traditional social work with disabled people? *Disability and Society*, 23 (3): 283–6.

Sandel, M (2010) *Justice: What's the right thing to do?* London: Penguin.

Sanderson, H (2000) *Person centred planning: Key features and approaches.* York: Joseph Rowntree Foundation.

Schön, D (1986) *Educating the reflective practitioner.* Oxford: Jossey-Bass.

SCIE/King's Fund (2011) *At a glance 45: Social care and clinical commissioning for people with long-term conditions.* London: SCIE.

Scragg, T and Mantell, A (eds) (2011) *Safeguarding adults in social work* (2nd edn). Exeter: Learning Matters.

Shaping Our Lives, National Centre for Independent Living and University of Leeds Centre for Disability Studies. (2007) *People management knowledge review 17. Developing social care: Service users driving culture change.* London: SCIE.

Slay, J (2011) *Budgets and beyond: Interim report.* London: SCIE/NEF.

Smale, G, Tuson, G, Biehal, N and Marsh, P (1993) *Empowerment, assessment, care management and the skilled worker.* London: NISW/HMSO.

Smith, B and Sparkes, A (2005) Men, sport, spinal cord injury and narratives of hope. *Social Science and Medicine*, 61: 1095–105.

Smith, B and Sparkes, A (2008) Narrative and its potential contribution to disability studies. *Disability and Society*, 23 (1): 17–28.

Smull, M and Sanderson, H (2005) *Essential lifestyle planning for everyone.* London: Inclusion Press.

Social Enterprise UK (2013) *What are social enterprises?* **www.socialenterprise.org.uk/**.

Stephens, L and Michaelson, J (2013) *Buying things together: A review of the up2us approach – Supporting people to pool budgets to buy the support they want.* London: NEF.

Stevenson, O (1996) *Elder protection in the community: What can we learn from child protection?* London: Age Concern Institute of Gerontology, Kings College.

Swain, J, Finklestein, V, French, S and Oliver, M (eds) (1993) *Disabling barriers – Enabling environments.* London: Sage Publications in association with the Open University.

Thomas, C (1999) Narrative identity and the disabled self, in Corker, M and French, S (eds) *Disability and discourse.* Milton Keynes: Open University Press.

Thomas T, Marshall, T and Bottomore, T (1992) *Citizenship and social class.* London: Pluto Press.

Thompson, N (2005) *Understanding social work: Preparing for practice* (2nd edn). Basingstoke: Palgrave Macmillan.

Thompson, N (2006) *Anti-discriminatory practice.* Basingstoke: Palgrave Macmillan.

Think Local Act Personal (2011) *Making it real: Marking progress towards personalised, community based support.* London: TLAP.

Think Local Act Personal (2013a) *National Personal Budgets Survey.* London: TLAP.

Think Local Act Personal (2013b) *The POET surveys of personal health budget holders and carers.* London: TLAP.

The College of Social Work (2012) *Curriculum guide: Personalisation.* London: The College of Social Work. **www.tcsw.org.uk/professional – development/educators/ curriculum**

Todd, L (2006) Enabling practice for professionals: The need for post-structuralist theory, in Goodley, D and Lawthorn, R (eds) *Disability and psychology*. Basingstoke: Palgrave Macmillan.

Tyson, A, Brewis, R, Crosby, N, Hatton, C, Stansfield, J, Tomlinson, C, Waters, J and Wood, A (2010) *A report on In Control's third phase: Evaluation and learning 2008–2009*. London: In Control.

UPIAS (1976) *Fundamental principles of disability*. London: UPIAS.

Vickers, T, Craig, G and Atkin, K (2012) Addressing ethnicity in social care research. *Social Policy and Administration*, 47 (3): 310–26.

Waters, J. (2011) *Community fund holding: A model for local choice and control*. Wythall: In Control.

Weaver, B and McNeill, F (2007) *Giving up crime: Directions for policy*. Glasgow School of Social Work and Scottish Centre for Crime and Justice Research. **www.sccjr.ac.uk/wp-content/uploads/2008/11/Giving_Up_Crime_tcm8-2569.pdf**.

Welsh Assembly Government (2000) *In safe hands: Implementing Adult Protection Procedures in Wales*. Cardiff: Welsh Assembly Government.

Welsh Assembly Government (2011) *Sustainable social services for Wales: A framework for action*. Cardiff: Welsh Assembly Government.

Williams, B and Tyson, A (2010) Self-direction, place and community: Re-discovering the emotional depths. A conversation with social workers in a London borough. *Journal of Social Work Practice*, 24 (3): 319–33.

Wolfensberger, W (1972) *The principle of normalization in human services*. Toronto: National Institute on Mental Retardation.

Wolfensberger, W (1983) Social role valorization: A proposed new term for the principle of normalization. *Mental Retardation*, 21 (6): 234 –9.

Zarb, G and Nadesh, P (1994) *Cashing in on independence: Comparing the costs and benefits of cash and services*. London: British Council of Disabled People (BCODP).

Website

www.supportplanning.org (2006) Thinking about support planning. London: Support Planning.

Index